Joseph B. Killebrew

Mineral and Agricultural Resources of the Portion of Tennessee

Along the Cincinnati Southern and Knoxville and Ohio Railroads

Joseph B. Killebrew

Mineral and Agricultural Resources of the Portion of Tennessee
Along the Cincinnati Southern and Knoxville and Ohio Railroads

ISBN/EAN: 9783337236939

Printed in Europe, USA, Canada, Australia, Japan

Cover: Foto ©Andreas Hilbeck / pixelio.de

More available books at **www.hansebooks.com**

MINERAL AND AGRICULTURAL RESOURCES

OF

THE PORTION OF TENNESSEE

ALONG THE

Cincinnati Southern and Knoxville & Ohio Railroads,

INCLUDING

THE COUNTRY BETWEEN THE TWO.

BY

J. B. KILLEBREW,

Commissioner of Agriculture, Statistics and Mines.

NASHVILLE:
TAVEL, EASTMAN & HOWELL.
1876.

To His Excellency, Gov. James D. Porter:

I have received from various parts of the United States, and especially from Europe, inquiries about the region traversed by the Cincinnati Southern Railroad. To meet this demand for information, and thus "attract capital and labor to the State," I have spent several months in studying the country on both sides of the railway, its mineral resources and agricultural capabilities, and have embodied the results of my observations in the accompanying pamphlet.

I have the honor to be,

Very respectfully,

J. B. KILLEBREW.

MINERAL AND AGRICULTURAL RESOURCES

OF THE PORTION OF TENNESSEE ALONG THE

CINCINNATI SOUTHERN RAILROAD.

The Cincinnati Southern Railroad has been a favorite project of leading capitalists, citizens and engineers of Cincinnati and central Kentucky, for many years. It was probably first discussed in 1834. In 1837 Colonel W. A. Gunn, the present engineer in charge of surveys on the road, made a partial survey of a road leading from Cincinnati in the general direction of Chattanooga. It is a remarkable fact, and no small compliment to Colonel Gunn, that his judgment of forty years ago has been substantially approved and adopted as the line of the road now approaching completion. In those early days, and ever since, the lion in the path which has deterred private capital from undertaking this great work, has been the Cumberland Mountain, whose rugged peaks have repelled any but the rudest civilization from an area nearly a hundred miles wide over which the route passes. To link Ohio, Indiana, Michigan, Western New York, and Pennsylvania to the great mineral region and rich cotton belt of the South, by a line almost as straight as the bird flies, the iron chain must be dragged through the bowels of the everlasting hills, over dizzy chasms, through a trackless, forbidding wilderness. Much of this region in Southern Kentucky and Northern Tennessee lacks only the Indian, the grizzly and the snows to rival the Sierras of the North as a barrier to engineering skill and a terrifier of railroad investors. To say that Cincinnati has shown daring enterprise in the expenditure of $16,000,000 to span this dividing wall between Northern and Southern products, is faintly expressing the truth. No city in the civilized world ever voluntarily made such a venture in behalf of her own commerce and the upbuilding of her interdependent neighbors. Never was such a magnificent endowment so skillfully and honestly expended, in the history of American internal improvements. No channel of commerce on the continent connects more important interests, and now has developed more "local" trade, than this will do.

The agitation which finally took concrete form in this subject began just after the war—perhaps we might say it was renewed then—by a half dozen enterprising men in Cincinnati, and as many more in Chattanooga. Projects without number were discussed and abandoned. The objective point, however, was kept steadily in view. Gradually all schemes centered in one to build the road *by* Cincinnati *for* Cincinnati, and in the interests of commerce, as distinguished from the interests of boards of directors. The Constitution of Ohio had to be flanked in the enabling act. That done, the Southern charters were still to procure. The Judiciary Committee in our own House of Representatives displayed hostility. The committee was voted down. Then a two years' siege was required to carry the works with which powerful interests had circumvallated the Legislature of Kentucky. One by one all these obstacles of men's creating gave way before the determined men who were managing the interest of Cincinnati. Meantime her citizens had voted ten millions of money with which to begin the work. These gigantic tasks were fairly begun in 1868. It required five years to complete the wordy preliminaries, and remove all the hindrances which written, and spoken eloquence could put in the way.

The first contract was for boring Kings Mountain tunnel, sections 57 and 58, in Kentucky. It was signed December 12, 1873. Since then the work of grading and otherwise preparing the road-bed has been vigorously pushed. The trustees expect to finish the line ready for the cars—excepting sideings and depots—by June 1, 1877.

The road is 336 41-100 miles long. Its general direction is north and south. The northern end bisects the Blue Grass region of Kentucky. The southern end, for about ninety miles, runs through a series of valleys that in fertility, beauty of scenery and healthful climate are not surpassed in Southern France or Italy. The middle section traverses a region rich, beyond the comprehension of the unskilled observer, in latent resources of mineral and agricultural products. Millions of acres on either side of the road, from the Kentucky River to Emory Gap, can be bought at merely nominal figures, but they are as good sheep lands, as good for the purposes of the grape culturist or general fruiterer, as any acres the sun shines on; while beneath them lie exhaustless beds of coal and iron in such close proximity as are found nowhere else in the world outside the Southern mineral region. When these dreary knobs are covered with vineyards and orchards and studded with sheep cotes; when scores of furnaces light up the gloomy ravines and impart their glow to the forbidding palisades, then will the great and enterprising city find that that which deterred all others from undertaking to build her a highway to the South brings her most profit; that these mountain fastnesses were better worth the reaching than the sunny plains beyond, covered with cotton and cane.

The principal southern connections of the Cincinnati road at its southern terminus will be the Western and Atlantic from Chattanooga to Atlanta, and connecting thence with Augusta, Macon, Savannah, Columbus, Pensacola, Brunswick, Jacksonville; and the Alabama and Chattanooga road from Chattanooga to Meridian, Mississippi, and connecting along the line and from its southern terminus with Montgomery, Mobile, Selma, Vicksburg, New Orleans, &c. The last mentioned is a natural and very important connection and link of the Southern Pacific Railway, destined to be completed at no distant day. When built, it must place Cincinnati on an equal footing, with reference to commercial intercourse with the Pacific slope, with St. Louis and Chicago. Indeed, she must be more eligibly situated than either of them, for her access will be quite as direct and always available for its highest capacity in freight or passenger traffic, whereas the Northern Pacific route, on which her rivals depend, is precarious during four months of the year from deep snows and severe cold. But we can not go into detail here. Let the reader take any map of the United States, and in the absence of the laid down line of the Cincinnati Southern, let him lay a string or rule from Cincinnati to Chattanooga, and study the strategic advantages gained by the former city with her road finished. Let him consider that every point named here has been placed as near to Cincinnati as it is now to Louisville. No thoughtful man can fail to comprehend the splendid field opened to the enterprise which conceived and executed the gigantic undertaking of reaching that field over its own railway.

By the construction of a branch railroad, beginning six miles south of the Tennessee and Kentucky State line, so as to connect at Careyville with the Knoxville and Ohio Railroad, now built out twenty-eight miles northward from Knoxville, Knoxville will be within 272 miles of Cincinnati, instead of 558 miles as now by the shortest railroad route built. Another proposed branch will unite the road with the Cumberland and Ohio, so as to bring Nashville within 291 miles of Cincinnati.

For seventy miles the Tennessee River runs parallel with the Cincinnati Southern, which will be a perpetual guarantee against high local freights, through the best part of the agricultural and mineral region through which it passes.

The road is probably the best built of any on the continent. The grades are lighter than those of any trunk line in the South. The highest curve permitted is 6°. Sixty-five per cent. of the line is straight. There are two and one-fifth miles of iron bridging, building and to be built, and but a thousand feet of wooden bridging. Three miles of iron viaduct are to be constructed over mountain streams. The tests applied to the iron and steel for the track, and to the iron columns and struts entering into the construction of bridges and viaducts, are the highest ever attempted in the history of American engineering, and they have been rigorously enforced in every instance. Steel rails are being laid on all the heavier grades. Steel rails only, will be used in the mountains. The iron rails furnished are nearly or quite equal to the ordinary run of steel rails. The heavy character of the mountain grading may be judged of from the fact that in less than 100 miles there are 4 85-100 miles of tunnel, much of it through a shale almost as hard as flint, but too much broken to serve for walls, and therefore requiring heavy timbering. It is doubtful if, when finished, any equal number of miles of road in the Union will have legitimately cost as much as this.

The following table shows the height of some principal points along the line above sea level, and their approximate distances from Chattanooga:

Name of Place.	Above Sea Level. Feet.	Distance from Chattanooga. Miles.
Chattanooga	685	0
Smith's X Roads, Tenn	709	27
Rockwood, Tenn	854	65
Emory Gap, Tenn	792	75
Triplett's Gap, Tenn	1209	90
Nix Creek, Tenn. (highest point on the line)	1518	112
Chitwoods, Tenn	1320	133
First Summit Cumberland Mountain, Ky	1257	145
Cumberland River, Ky	745	158
King's Mountain, Ky	1287	195
Danville, Ky	955	235
Kentucky River, Ky	767	240
Lexington, Ky	966	260
Ohio River Bridge	537	336

The general importance of the Cincinnati Southern Railway consists in the fact that it is part of a great South and North system, now in its infancy, but destined to become, during this century, quite equal in importance to the system connecting the Eastern sea-board with the agricultural region of the West. Already the Louisville and Nashville road and its connections has exploded the postulate that "none but east and west lines can be made to pay." It and its fellow, connecting the two principal entrepots of trade in the Ohio valley with the cotton, rice and sugar fields of the gulf belt, are a nucleus that will expand into a power destined, at no distant period, to turn the course of commerce and work profound social, political and economical revolutions. This South and North system, being comparatively short, will solve the Granger's question—"How shall I reach the best market"—by bringing the market to his door. It will do more; it will create demand, as well as supply that which exists. The population depending on it in the South will increase as rapidly as that of the North-west has in the last four decades under the influence of the East and West system.

It is fortunate for Tennessee that she lies in the track of

and has within her borders the main termini of the two successful trunk lines connecting the North with the South. The Louisville and Nashville, in its operations, has been worth millions to Middle and West Tennessee. The Cincinnati Southern will be equally beneficial to the Eastern and Southern portions of the State. The two lines, when the latter is completed (the Louisville and Nashville is capitalized at $27,000,000), will wield an actual capital of about $60,000,000! They place Tennessee, relatively, in the position Ohio occupies with reference to the New York Central and Baltimore and Ohio. We are the grand entrepot for the cotton belt trading to the North, and the distributing point for the North trading to the South. Add to this the fact that—the East and North-west having more roads than they can make profitable—railroad building for a quarter of a century will be confined to North and South lines, and it requires no prophetic vision to realize more than all the most enthusiastic friends of the South may predict for her, as to future development in agricultural and manufacturing progress and increase in wealth and population. The railroad system we have described is destined to be the great pacificator, educator, liberalizer and enriching force of the Mississippi Valley. Tennessee starts in the race at least ten years in advance of her Southern sisters. May she be found worthy of her high trust, equal to the realization of her great advantages.

General View of the Route.

Our purpose in this report is to give some account of the resources, so far as Tennessee is concerned, as well as the geological and topographical features, of the country lying on the route.

The entire length of the road from Chattanooga to the

Kentucky State line is 136 miles, eighty miles of which are along one of the minor parallel valleys of the Valley of East Tennessee which lie at the south-eastern foot of the Cumberland Table-land. At Emory Gap the line of the road leaves the Valley of East Tennessee and begins to ascend the mountain, and throughout the remaining fity-six miles the road cuts through the coal formation. The Valley of East Tennessee, which lies between the Unaka range on the south-east and the Cumberland Table-land on the north-west, is made up of a succession of minor ridges and valleys, running in almost unbroken lines in a north-easterly and south-westerly direction. Viewed from the higher points of the Unaka range, or from the top of the Cumberland Table-land, the minor ridges melt into a common plain. The average elevation of the Valley of East Tennessee is about 1,000 feet above the sea, while that of the Table-land is 2,000 feet. Prof. Lesley, of Pennsylvania, thinks the preservation of our coal-fields is due to a great downthrow fault, by which the whole of our coal-fields were sunk several thousand feet below their original elevation. The sections which retained their altitude have been eroded of all their coal measures and of the formations immediately below the coal measures, so that the Upper Silurian of the valley lies almost in juxtaposition to the coal measures, though separated geologically by an immense period. This theory is rendered probable from the fact that the strata of Walden's Ridge, which runs parallel with the Cumberland Table-land, are highly inclined, indeed sometimes vertical, or even beyond verticality, making the line of a great fault, caused by the downthrow of the Cumberland Table-land. This geological event is one that has an important bearing upon the value of the mineral region immediately adjacent to the line of railroad. By it the coal and iron are placed side by side, ready for profitable working. The fossil iron ore of the Clinton group runs in almost unbroken lines from Chattanooga to Emory Gap on the line of road, while the outcrops of coal on the Cumberland Table-land a few furlongs distant are persistent. Associated in the same group are the carboniferous limestones, which form an excellent flux, and at a short distance the Trenton limestones of the Lower Silurian. Besides these, the sandstones of the coal measures are found in many instances, suitable for making furnace hearths. It would be difficult in any State to find more of the materials for the manufacture of iron in such proximity. And as the construction of the railroad will furnish the only thing lacking—transportation—the intelligent prediction of Prof. Lesley in regard to this region will doubtless be realized, when he says: "A thousand collieries will be started in the mountain, and a thousand iron works will be established on the ores at its foot; a thousand villages, towns and cities will grow up in the broad limestone plain before it; a thousand factories and mills will make these towns hum with life, and all this life will base itself on the mountain coal thus wonderfully preserved from destruction by throes of the earth in ancient days, which would have obliterated every trace of human life from the continent, had the divine invention of human life been made." The small valleys lying on the east side of the railroad, numbering from two to three, between the line of the road and the river, rest upon the magnesian limestone of the Knox formation. The ridges between the valleys are composed of the chert and shales of the same formation. The hills have a thin barren soil, covered usually with a small growth of timber, and the soil is not of sufficient fertility to repay the labor of the husbandman. The valleys are usually fertile, gently undulating, and form the only arable land in the vicinity of the road. These valleys will average in width about half a mile. They are thickly settled, and are for the most part cleared up. The timber supply is on the ridges. The mountain slopes supply good lumbering trees, which will be described more in detail hereafter.

Between Emory Gap and the Kentucky State line the soil is derived from sandstone, is thin and unproductive of the usual field crop. Not one acre in twenty has been brought into cultivation. The Cumberland Table-land loses much of its plateau character in this portion of the State. The surface is usually rugged, with high, sharp-crested ridges and rounded peaks, that sometimes rise 1,500 feet above the road-bed. Though rugged, the country is well timbered, and on the northern slopes of the ridges the soil is very fertile, and the timber of excellent quality. Deep, canyon-like gorges are cut by the numerous streams deep in the bosom of the mountain. Some of these streams are walled in by perpendicular cliffs of sandstone from 300 to 400 feet high. A few narrow valleys occur between the foot of the superimposed ridges, but these mountain valleys are not so productive as the northern and western slopes of the ridges.

From these high mountain sides many fine chalybeate and other springs break out. Wild grasses spring up in great abundance and supply a rich forage for cattle and sheep. The air is pure and the region healthy. For the growth of apples no region is superior to the country which lies between Emory Gap and the Kentucky State line. They never fail, and they have a plumpness and richness of flavor rarely equalled.

To sum up in brief the advantages which the country on this portion of the line affords, we may say:

1. It is healthy. Consumption is almost unknown here, and malarious diseases seldom occur. In many places there are no doctors within twenty miles. The inhabitants are hardy and long-lived, though living a life of privation and exposure.

2. It has an abundance of coal. Throughout the extent

of the railroad from Emory Gap to the Kentucky State line every cut reveals more or less coal. The seams are sometimes thin and worthless, but often are from three to four feet thick. In the ridges above the road better and thicker seams are met with.

3. It has a great variety of valuable timber. For many miles the line of road traverses forests of the finest white oak. On the mountain slopes are poplar and walnut in great quantity. From Scott and Morgan counties timber enough to supply all the agricultural implement manufactories within reach of the road for a century to come, can be obtained.

4. The forests of chestnut oak which are usually found upon the tops of the ridges are very extensive, and are capable of supplying millions of cords of the very best tan-bark.

5. As a grazing region it is very valuable. The wild grasses are everywhere abundant, and great herds of cattle are fattened upon these wild grasses for the Northern markets. Goats, that thrive upon shrubbery, can be reared at nominal cost. They live throughout the winter without any other food than the buds of the native shrubs. Sheep also are very hardy and do well.

6. An excellent situation for extensive apple orchards. The apple is the surest crop grown, and the facilities which the road will afford, together with the small outlay necessary to start an orchard, will make this a famous region for the production of apples, and will enable it to compete successfully with any portion of the United States.

7. As a place for summer resort it must become famous. The salubrity of the air, the excellence of the chalybeate springs, the high elevation, and the grandeur and beauty of the natural scenery, will make it a favorite locality for those accustomed to such rural retreats in summer.

8. For growing all garden vegetables the soil of this

sandstone formation is well adapted. Early vegetables can be supplied to the Cincinnati and other markets at a cheaper rate than from any other point. Irish potatoes, cabbage, onions, and indeed all root crops, grow to great perfection. The Irish potatoes especially are noted for their excellence. Market gardening will doubtless become one of the leading industries of this mountain region.

FROM CHATTANOOGA TO NORTH CHICAMAUGA.

Such is a general view of the country bordering the Cincinnati Southern Railroad. For the purpose of entering into details, we return to Chattanooga, and, crossing the upper ferry, we find a series of low ridges lying on the right, from which the *dyestone,* or *fossil red hematite,* has been dug for many years. The place of mining is not more than one mile north-east of Chattanooga, and the ore is found in what is called Stringer's Hill, the third of the series of ridges from Walden's Ridge. Walden's Ridge is an arm of the Cumberland Table-land, and is eight miles across. It is separated from the main plateau by Sequatchee Valley on the west. The mining in Stringer's Hill has been carried on in the head of a decapitated fold, the strata here all dipping to the south-east at an angle of 22 degrees. The iron ore, fifteen inches thick, is found associated with shales, several thin partings being found in the seam. This ore is soft and its value impaired by the commingling shale. The seam can be traced many miles to the north-east, but is finally cut out by the valley of North Chicamauga. It may be here mentioned that the railroad crosses Tennessee river four miles above Chattanooga, and keeps the valley of North Chicamauga until it reaches the Tennessee Valley. This ore is therefore not on the line of the road, but is sufficiently near the river, which serves all purposes of transportation. Crossing a low gap in Moccasins ridge going north, we enter Tennessee Valley, which extends as far as Emory Gap, a distance of eighty miles. Bounding this valley on the west is a low ridge known as Shin Bone, which separates the Tennessee Valley from Back Valley, lying next to the escarpment of Walden's Ridge. Back Valley and Tennessee Valley become one near the point where North Chicamauga breaks from the mountain. The united valleys are one and a half miles wide, presenting a magnificent farming area.

The first coal of importance that presents itself is on Walden's Ridge, eight miles north-west of Chattanooga and quite as far from the railroad, though within three miles of the Tennessee River. It belongs to the upper coal measures, and outcrops at the foot of a ridge 110 feet high, which rests upon the general level of the Table-land, which is here 1,000 feet high. This ridge extends towards the north several miles and is about half a mile wide, supplying a large body of coal. The seam is three and a half feet thick, and an entry has been driven in at the eastern foot for the distance of fifty yards. Some 15,000 bushels of coal have been taken out and hauled in wagons down the mountain to Chattanooga. It is a hard, free-burning coal, though containing some sulphur. Underlying it are several feet of good fire-clay. The roof is of black shale, and is quite solid. All the strata are horizontal. The mine is known as Crow's bank. If proper facilities were afforded for conveying the coal to the valley below, this mine, owing to its proximity to Chattanooga, would doubtless prove very valuable. At present the cost of mining and transportation to market is nearly equal to the selling price.

Below the bank on the South is the cliffy rampart that makes such a prominent and striking feature in the escarpment of the Table-land. Underlying this cliff rock another seam appears, three and a half feet thick. The coal is very hard. This could be taken out by the river, which is about two and a half miles south. Other seams of unknown thickness are seen along the bluffs, some of them having been worked to a limited extent during the civil war, and the coal taken to Chattanooga on barges. On the opposite side of the river, in Raccoon mountain, are numerous seams of coal, which have been worked at the Ætna and Vulcan mines for many years. A description of these mines is reserved for another part of this work.

It has already been stated that Back Valley and the Tennessee Valley become one where the Chicamauga breaks from the mountain. The gulf made by the Chicamauga is deep and wide, forming a chasm much like an inverted roof, though sometimes the bluffs of sandstone rise boldly up for several hundred feet. Rogers' creek, which is a tributary of Chicamauga, makes also a deep chasm in the mountain, parallel with Tennessee Valley, leaving a high, narrow headland between it and the valley, which narrows to a sharp ridge where the waters of Rogers' creek and Chicamauga unite. Each one of these chasms exposes the coal seams and makes them accessible. Branch railroads may be constructed up these gorges, so that the coal may, by chutes, be dumped directly into the cars.

Fallingwater, another stream tributary to North Chicamauga, and south of Rogers' creek, rises upon the plateau of Walden's Ridge and flows in an easterly direction, making a gorge of increasing width and depth as it approaches Back Valley. Reaching this it turns north, running about a mile, when it cuts through Back Valley and Shin Bone Ridge, passing in a south-easterly direction through Tennessee Valley into North Chicamauga. The point of its confluence with the latter stream is ten miles (north, 20 degrees east) from Chattanooga. Where Fallingwater breaks through Shin Bone Ridge there is a bluff which shows an antilineal fold, the rocks dipping at an average angle of 32 degrees to the north-west and southeast. In the south-west dip several seams of dyestone ore are seen interstratified with a shale highly calcareous. A section taken at this place, beginning at the lowest exposed strata and ascending, shows:

Shale..	25 feet.
Dyestone ore...	9 inches.
Shale and flaggy sandstones.....................	1 foot.
Dyestone ore...	13 inches.
Shale	2.6 feet.
Dyestone ore...	6 inches.
Shale...	4 feet.
Dyestone ore...	4 inches.
Shale, brownish..	6 feet.
Dyestone ore...	6 inches.
Shales and sandstones, thin and flaggy, above.	

The specimens of iron ore taken from this place show a large amount of siliceous matter. The ore contains but few fossils, and is very hard. It has never been used in any furnace.

By the confluence of Fallingwater with North Chicamauga a sufficient volume of water is obtained to run machinery. Two mills are in operation between this point and the mouth of North Chicamauga. Ascending the gulf cut by Fallingwater to the mouth of Mill creek, and turning up the latter stream, several good seams of coal are seen. Going to the top of Walden's Ridge and descending, the first outcrop is found two hundred yards on the north side of Mill creek, in the head of a cross ravine, the water from which passes down Rogers' creek, a tributary of North Chicamauga. The coal at the outcrop is one foot thick, but increases to eighteen inches by going in twelve feet. The seam is horizontal, with black shale below and soft, blue shale above. The coal is hard, lustrous, and cubical, of excellent quality, and free from iron pyrite. It belongs to the upper measures, the conglomerate appearing lower down on the mountain, and may be the equivalent of the Sewanee seam. The distance of this coal from the railroad is two miles.

Passing now in our descent from the mountain in a southerly direction over the dividing ridge between the headwaters of Rogers' creek and Mill creek, another seam ninety-five feet below has been opened on the south side of Mill creek. The coal at this place is spurmous and porous, but free from sulphur. The seam dips gently to the south, is two and a half feet thick, with a good hard slate roof and sandstone bottom. The same seam has been opened two hundred yards further down the stream. The difference in level is very slight, as shown by the barometer, not more than four or five feet, which the dip of the strata here will readily account for. The coal at this latter opening (Wilkerson's) is one foot thick at the outcrop, increasing to 2.3 feet at the distance of forty feet, which is as far as the gangway has been driven. Overlying it is a gray slate, and beneath three feet of fire-clay, which rests upon a bed of sandstone. This seam lies included between two layers of conglomerate rock, one 200 feet above and the other 40 feet below. It is doubtless the same seam which is interpolated in the lower conglomerate in White county and other places.

By far the most interesting development of coal on the waters of Mill Creek is seen a quarter of a mile below Wilkerson's Bank, on the opposite side of the stream. The coal here appears under the thick sandstone cliff 194 feet below Wilkerson's. The sandstone immediately above the coal is about 60 feet in thickness, with a superimposed back bench of sandstone 80 feet thick. At the outcrop this coal is 21 inches in thickness, with 14 inches of soft, shaly sandstone below. Still beneath this is a hard white sandstone. The soft bed of sandstone disappears at the distance of 30 yards, and a black bituminous shale takes its place. The coal also increases to 39 inches. The top consists of a hard, ferruginous sandstone, with no shale. The surface is in waves, with occasionally heavy swells and flat convexities, giving the coal a variable thickness. Near the termination of the entry, which is 96 feet long, there is a slight uplift in the floor, of a foot, and a much greater one in the roof. The entry dips at the rate of three inches to the yard.

This seam unquestionably corresponds with the cliff seam as found on the western side of the Cumberland Table-land. (See Little Sequatchee Coal Field.) The coal taken from the entry presents a singular aspect. It is semi-lustrous and porous. The laminæ are well defined, but are curved and rolled into an infinite number of plications, showing at the same time a fibrous structure undisturbed across the general plane of lamination, very much like ice half melted in the sun, splitting easily across the laminated surface into basaltiform or columnar masses. It comes out in great blocks, and presents a handsome appearance. About 1,000 bushels have been mined at this point, and the product used in the neighboring blacksmith shops, where it is greatly prized for its excellent welding and heating properties.

The descent to the line of railroad, one and a half miles distant, is rapid. To the valley below, half a mile, there is a fall of between 700 and 800 feet. From the bottom, just below the mine, to the railroad, the surface is level. To convey the coal to the railroad, therefore, an incline would be required to carry it to the foot of the mountain, and from thence by a switch to the main track.

One hundred and thirty-two feet below this cliff seam is the outcrop of another seam 14 inches thick. This is capped by 20 feet of siliceous brown and black shales, with two feet of fire clay beneath the coal, resting upon sandstone. The quality of the coal from this seam can hardly be determined, as only the crumbling outcrop has been taken out. The specimens I saw are not so compact as those from the cliff seam above, but resemble the Rockwood coal, being fragile, shelly and soft, showing no columnar structure. Some thin seams of mineral charcoal are found interlaminated with it, and also some specimens exhibiting a beautiful irridescence. The laminæ are considerably disturbed, and are easily separable, showing a surface which glistens like highly polished leather. It is clean, and comparatively free from sulphur. The same seam has been worked to a limited extent on the southern side of the creek, where it shows a thickness of 18 inches, with a tendency to a greater thickness as the entry is extended.

The plateau and slopes of the mountain above are well wooded. Pine, white oak, red oak and chestnut are abundant on the plateau, while upon the margin of the streams poplar, hemlock, maple, black gum and holly are seen. The steep slopes to the valley abound with good lumber trees. The soil of the valleys, once very productive, has been much injured by overcropping, and by a want of proper rest, rotation and clovering. Many of the slopes are worn down to the red clay, and their fertility utterly destroyed. These places show with a painful prominence. Corn, oats, and wheat are the principal crops grown in the valley, but the yield is not more than half as great as when the land was fresh. Thirty bushels per acre are considered a good yield for corn, ten for wheat and twenty-five for oats. With a judicious system of tillage these yields might be largely increased. Corn forms almost the sole article of export, with the exception of dried fruit, eggs, feathers and butter. Ginseng is found in the mountain coves to a limited extent, but the product is yearly diminishing.

From North Chicamauga to Soddy Creek Mines.

Crossing the North Chicamauga near the location of the railroad bridge, and ascending the mountain by a very steep pathway on the left, we get first upon a bench about two-thirds of the way to the top of the mountain. The surface of this bench is covered with a luxuriant growth of wild grasses in summer, which supply ample forage for great herds of cattle. The woods are open, no underbrush anywhere obstructing the view. The overlooking bluffs are of shelving sandstones, where many rock houses are seen—natural shelters for stock against the heats of summer or the chill winds of winter. Reaching the top of the mountain, which is here, as measured by the barometer, 1,134 feet above the valley, we find the surface very level and well timbered with chestnut oak. The conglomerate rocks are everywhere displayed, sometimes rising up above the surface in great masses, the erosion curving them into many fantastic shapes. This stretch of level land extends from the gorge of the North Chicamauga to Soddy Creek, about eight miles, with scarcely a break that would interfere with the construction of a railroad. The soil on this plateau is rather better than most of the soil of the Table-land. On Poe's turnpike, which forms the highway from Dunlap in Sequatchee Valley, across Walden's Ridge to the Tennessee Valley, a few farms of moderate fertility are met with. Upon these farms are grown wheat, sorghum, corn, oats, Irish potatoes, beans, cabbage, and garden vegetables generally. The soil, however, is not well adapted to the growth of Indian corn and sorghum. Apple trees flourish, are long-lived, and bear well. Peaches, it is said, do better here than on the western side of the mountain. Herds grass springs up spontaneously, and is the main reliance of farmers for hay. Clover, by the application of a small quantity of gypsum, proves a profitable crop, both as a fertilizer and for grazing. Upon clover sod a fair crop of Indian corn or wheat may be grown. Some good farmers upon the plateau make from twenty to thirty bushels of corn per acre, though the usual average is not above six or eight. The timber supply is ample. Large white oaks, easily rived, and of a toughness that makes the timber of especial value for the wagon-maker, are numerous. Yellow pines two and a half feet in diameter are found in clusters. Chestnut, chestnut oak, red oak, black oak, and gum grow everywhere in profusion. Walnut occurs in the coves, and sometimes, though rarely, upon the top of the mountain. Chinquapins and chestnuts are so abundant as to form articles of export.

On this charming plateau between North Chicamauga and Soddy a curious lake occurs, not far from the northern bank of the Chicamauga. A ridge, elevated considerably above the general level, overlooks the Chicamauga gulf on the south. Half a mile north of this ridge there has been a drop in the mountain, exposing a perpendicular sandstone bluff 100 feet high. The lake lies at the foot of this bluff, and is deeply set in the bosom of the mountain. In shape it is elliptical, and resembles a large tureen embedded in the plateau. The water is at least fifty feet below the top of the surrounding bluffs, and the edge of the water can be reached only by a precipitous path on the eastern side. The lake is 100 yards in its longest diameter, and about 75 yards in its shortest. Its depth is unknown. No rude plummet of the mountaineer has ever been able to fathom its waters, though many attempts have been made. The water is very cold, and of a sky blue color. It never becomes muddy, even in a rainy season. It has no perceptible outlet or inlet. During the dry months in summer the water recedes some two or three feet, leaving exposed a narrow rocky beach next to the steep walls that environ it. The surface of these walls is beautifully scolloped by the motion of the water. Viewed from above it appears motionless, and looks as though no wind could ever ruffle its calm, clear surface. No fish disport in its waters, and yet it would seem to be a very paradise for the trout, for the rearing of which it will no doubt in time be utilized.

North Chicamauga has several tributaries from the north. Among them are Hog Pen Branch, Four Mile Branch, Yellow Spring, Cooper Creek, Panther Creek, and Cane Creek. These streams have cut deep furrows in the mountain which are difficult to pass. They are from one hundred to five hundred feet deep. Up near their sources are some level bottoms bordering them, but most generally their banks are precipitous. Cane Creek, one of the largest tributaries of North Chicamauga, flows in a very deep, narrow chasm, much like a canyon. The bluffs are of sandstone, and often overhang their base fifteen or twenty feet. Talus has accumulated at the base of these bluffs so as to give a slope to the water's edge. This talus-slope is fringed by trees forming a green tortuous line in summer, several hundred feet below the general top of the plateau. When once in these gorges, one has to walk oftentimes many miles before any place of ascent can be found.

The process of erosion as shown in these bluffs furnishes a curious study. The water trickles down from above and enters the crevices of the rocks where they are often shaded by the jutting layers of sandstone. Here it freezes and acts as wedges, splitting off great slabs in vertical lines from the mountain mass. Often the exposed surface is covered with thin incrustations of the carbonate of lime, which has been deposited on the rocks by the trickling waters. From what source the waters become charged with calcareous matter it would be difficult to tell.

Coal crops out in many places in the gulf of North Chicamauga, showing three or four seams of workable thickness. At one place on Cane creek, three-quarters of a mile above its mouth, are some interesting objects. The bottom of the stream is covered with immense sandstone boulders, making its ascent exceedingly difficult even when the water is low enough to permit one to jump from rock to rock. At some points the masses of sandstone lie piled up in inextricable confusion, mingled with great drifts of dead timber, so as almost to bid defiance to any progress. At the distance from the mouth mentioned, a rock house occurs on the left bank, the floor of which is nearly level with the water. The roof at the outer edge is thirty feet high, but curves down to the floor at the distance of twenty yards or more. In this rock house is a small furnace stack, which the inhabitants say has existed beyond the memory of any person now living on the mountain. A fine chalybeate spring breaks out at the back part of this rock house, and traces of coal are met with where the floor and roof unite. The most noticeable feature, however, are the seams of coal interwoven with the conglomerate rock overhead. They run in every conceivable direction through the rock, as though boiled up with the sandstone when in a plastic state. Fossils of the *lepidodendron* and *siggillaria* present themselves all over the roof. The thickest coal seam is about one foot, and this runs in a wavy, twisting line through the mass of conglomerate.

It has already been mentioned that near the sources of these streams some wide bottoms occur. The soils of these bottoms differ from that of the plateau, in having more clay in their composition. In color these soils are gray; in consistency, waxy; and in constitution, heavy and cold. The timber indicates the difference in soils, being in the bottoms mostly poplar, pine, and the red flowering maple.

The grazing privileges of the plateau under consideration are very valuable. The earliest mountain grass appears about the 15th of April. This is the mountain sedge, and supplies good grazing until toughened by the heats of July and August. The golden rod, rich weed, wild tea, wild oats, beggars' lice, and some others, supply successive grazing crops until the first of October, when the wintergreen, a delicate grass with flat blades, not unlike the blue grass, comes up and keeps green throughout the winter.

It is not affected by the rigor of winter, and to its nutritious qualities much of the stock of the Table-land owe their means of surviving the winter. Cattle relish it, and prefer it to any other grass, though it is not so abundant as the mountain sedge.

SODDY CREEK MINES.

Soddy creek, a small tributary of the Tennessee river, has two forks, the more southern being called Little Soddy, and the more northern, Soddy, it being considered the main stream. Both of these branches have carved deep notches in the side of the mountain. On the side of the gulf formed by Little Soddy, six hundred yards from its confluence with the main stream, four miles west from the Tennessee, eighteen miles north-east of Chattanooga, and within half a mile of the line of railroad, the Soddy mines have been opened. The section, as taken here, shows eight seams of coal. Beginning at the top of the mountain on the north side of Little Soddy, and overlooking that stream, we have section on next page:

Coal. Thickness.	Section.	Name of Materials.	Ft.	In.
ft. in.		Surface..................	10	0
		Sandstone..............	83	0
2 4		Shale......................	1	3
		COAL.		
		Gray Shale.............	40	0
3 0		COAL.		
		Fire-clay.................	6	0
		Sandy Shale...........	20	0
1 6		COAL.		
		Sandy Shale...........	40	0
3 6		COAL.		
		Fire-clay.................	2	0
		Sandstone..............	100	0
		Shale......................	13	0
2 0		COAL.		
		Fire-clay.................	2	0
		Black Shale............	40	0
1 9		COAL.		
		Gray Shale.............	35	0
2 6		COAL.		
		Fire-clay.................	8	0
		Shaly Sandstone.....	40	0
1 9		COAL.		
		Sandstone..............	50	0
		Red Shale...............	18	0
		Mountain Limestone..	523	4

The fourth seam from the top is the one now worked, and has a slight dip to the west. Overlying the coal is a hard black shale, which makes a hard, solid and safe roof.

The main gangway is about 300 yards long. On the left are two cross entries, one of which extends to the distance of 350 yards, and the second about half as far. On the right there is only one cross entry, which is about 100 yards long. The rooms are worked sixteen yards wide, with road in the center, and slack or "gob" on each side. The general average of the seam is about three feet, making the amount of dead work, caused by taking up a part of the floor for the purpose of heightening the entries, cost about twenty-five cents to the ton of coal. The work is carried on by a system of pillars and rooms, the pillars being eight yards wide between the main entry and the room, with four yards between each room. The mines are drained by a syphon pipe, $2\frac{1}{2}$ inches in diameter. When the second entry shall have been driven in to unite with the first, the mines will drain themselves. Ventilation is effected by a furnace and shaft. A second entry has been made about fifty yards north of the main entry, and is eighty yards long. There is only one cross entry in this, ninety-six yards long, with nine rooms. In these rooms the coal will average three and a half feet thick, and sometimes reaches four feet or more. For driving main entries, eight feet wide and six feet high, $5.50 per yard is paid; for cross entries, five to seven feet, $3.50 per yard. The number of miners at present (December, 1876) employed in these mines is twenty-one, who raise an average of sixty bushels each per day. Nineteen other persons are employed as drivers, weighers, etc. The wages paid range from one dollar to two and a quarter per day. The amount of coal raised and shipped from September 1, 1875, to September 1, 1876, was 240,655 bushels. The amount for the year 1875 was 177,309; for 1876 to December 223,939. The estimated cost of mining is three cents per bushel, and the cost of getting it to market, in Chattanooga, about the same. The amount of capital invested is $20,000. The coal is taken down the mountain by an incline two hundred yards long, where it is dumped into a chute, and the larger cars beneath, holding each sixty-five bushels, are loaded. These are drawn by mules, on a tram-road three miles long, to a point on Soddy creek, where the coal is loaded in barges, holding 3,500 bushels each, and floated to Chattanooga. When the water is high the barges can be carried from the place of loading on Soddy creek to Chattanooga in six hours, but double that time is required in a low stage of water. This coal finds a ready market in Chattanooga, owing to its excellent quality. It is highly bituminous, burns with a bright, ruddy flame, and is a good binding coal. It shows in its structure but little lamination, but resembles blocks of pitch, with shining black specks.

The mine was originally leased by a company of twenty Welshmen, who agreed to pay a royalty of one cent per bushel. This company having failed, the property passed into the hands of a receiver. The royalty has been reduced to half a cent per bushel.

These mines are capable of indefinite expansion, and when the railroad shall be completed, they will become one of the most valuable coal properties in the State. About four acres of coal have been taken out, and the average per acre so far from one seam has been over 3,000 tons. Several seams above and below this have been thoroughly tested. The one immediately above is very free from impurities, and is preferred by blacksmiths.

Higher up the gorge of Little Soddy, about half a mile above the point now worked, the same seam has an outcrop of six feet two inches thick. The difficulty and outlay necessary to reach this place have prevented any work from being done.

A mining village has sprung up in the valley below the mines, beyond the line of railroad. It has a post-office, two stores, two schools, two churches, and a population of about two hundred.

The valley lying at the foot of the mountain at this place is a mile wide. Much of it near the mountain, however, is rendered comparatively worthless by the prevalence of large sandstones, that have tumbled down from the face of the mountain. In some places these sandstones have crumbled, by the action of the weather, leaving great thick layers of ferruginous sand, which is infertile. The cultivable portions of the bottoms are moderately productive. Herdsgrass, timothy and clover are sown for hay, which yield from one to one and a half tons per acre, clover making the largest yield and herdsgrass the least. The yield of corn per acre is 25 bushels; wheat, 10 bushels; oats, 35 bushels; sweet potatoes, 75 bushels; Irish potatoes, about 100 bushels. Nearly all the corn and hay are fed to cattle, and the latter are driven to Chattanooga.

After passing the village, Soddy creek cuts through a series of ridges nearly at right angles, making a bottom of moderate width to the Tennessee river. The bottoms on the latter stream are very wide, and of unbounded fertility. Probably there is no soil in any State that matures such large quantities of Indian corn. About 500,000 bushels are shipped annually from the different landings between Chattanooga and Kingston, nearly all of which is raised on the Tennessee bottoms and islands. The productiveness of these bottoms may be inferred from the fact that from fifteen to thirty bushels per acre is the rental price, the latter for island farms. Some of these island farms have been sold since the war for prices varying from $100 to $210 per acre. The overflows, which deposit a large amount of sediment, keep the soil in a high condition of fertility, and permit it to be cultivated every year without any apparent diminution in its productive capacity. Mr. Tom Crutchfield, who has a bottom farm four miles above Chattanooga, raised 120 bushels of corn to the acre. The annual average, however, on the best lowlands, is about seventy-five bushels. The great difference in the producing capacity of the Tennessee bottoms and those lying at the foot of the Cumberland Table-land, arises from their inherent difference in constitution. The former are fed by the limestone bluffs that overhang them, as well, as by the sedimentary deposits from the river; the latter have no new supplies of fertility. The cherty ridges on the east, and the sandstone bluffs on the west, are deficient in plant food, and the bottoms lying between lack the calcareous element so necessary to a prolific yield of the cereals.

A large proportion of the good timber of the valleys has been exhausted. The bounding ridges and mountain sides, however, supply it in any desirable quantity. The yellow pine is abundant. This is converted into lumber, and sold at the saw-mills at $15 per thousand; white oak, from $10 to $12.50 per thousand. A small quantity of walnut and ash are found in the coves of the mountains between Chattanooga and Soddy creek, but not in sufficient quantity to deserve special mention.

From Soddy Creek to Sale Creek.

This section includes a distance of twelve miles along the line of railroad. The first place worthy of notice is O'Possum creek, four miles above Soddy, which, though a wet weather stream, has left its deep gulf in the side of the mountain. It is also a tributary of the Tennessee, cutting its way, like Soddy creek, at right angles through the series of ridges lying between the mountain and Tennessee river. This stream exposes some fine seams of coal in the mountain gorges. One outcrop, within 20 feet of the stream bed, shows over two feet of good coal, which would doubtless become a three foot seam at a short distance. Two or more good exposures are found in the bluffs above. A small quantity has been taken out of the lowest seam for blacksmith purposes, and is said to be a very "strong" coal. At the outcrops the seams at this place are quite as promising as at Soddy creek, and a little prospecting would no doubt reveal excellent coal of good thickness. At one place near the crest of the mountain, on the right of the stream, the coal shows 3½ feet. Another promising outcrop is on Ritchee's branch, that runs north into O'Possum. The mountain here has not, however, as great an elevation as at Soddy by 150 feet, and the three higher seams are probably wanting. This would leave, however, the seam now worked at Soddy, which is doubtless the coal near the top, showing 3½ feet.

The topographical features of the section embraced between Soddy creek and O'Possum are slightly varied by the nearer approach of the parallel ridges. From comparatively flat bottoms below, with a U form, in this section they take a V shape, or are trough-like, with but a small quantity of arable land. The slopes of the ridges, where gentle in their acclivity, have been brought into cultivation, but they are scarcely more productive than the level mountain plateau 900 feet above. The geological continuity prevails here as lower down the valleys: the Knox chert on the ridges next the Tennessee river, and the Clinton or Dyestone group next to the mountain, though there is a noticeable absence of red fossil iron ore for many miles. Some few specimens of brown hematite are seen at the foot of the ridges, but it probably exists nowhere in this section in workable quantities.

The section made through the river ridges by O'Possum creek makes a bottom half mile wide and four miles long, with a soil much like that on Soddy creek, being largely intermixed with sand, having a yellowish cast, and interspersed with blocks of sandstone.

Sale Creek Mines.

These mines are situated nine miles north-east of Soddy on Rocky creek, a tributary of Sale creek, which empties into the Tennessee river. The operations at Sale Creek Mines are now suspended, and work will not be resumed until the completion of the Cincinnati Southern Railroad. Formerly the coal was carried by a tramway four and a half miles long to Sale creek, from which place it was floated in barges down the Tennessee river. These mines were successfully worked up to 1875, at which time a flood washed away the tram-road and bridges, so crippling the company that work was suspended. The topography of the region around these mines presents some singular features. Rocky creek runs out at right angles from a series of broken knobs bordering the main mountain, and empties into Sale creek one and a half miles below the mines. Near the base of the mountain it has three branches, one coming from the north, one from the south, and one from the west. These streams all unite back of the range of hills, and near the base of the mountain. The most southern, called Clemons creek, separates in part the southern outlying knob or ridge from Walden's Ridge. This outlying spur is known as Shin Bone ridge, though geologically it differs entirely from the ridge of the same name at Fallingwater, the latter belonging to the Clinton or Dyestone group, and the former to the coal formations. This ridge extends as far south as O'Possum creek, where it unites with Walden's Ridge. In Shin Bone ridge the coal has been worked in two places, one on the western and the other on the northern slope, facing Rocky creek. The seam worked in this ridge is four feet thick near the outcroop, but squeezes down in some places to one foot or less, and swelling out at times to six feet. The entries here were abandoned because of a fault. The general dip of the seam is slightly to the west, but throughout it shows much disturbance, as though the whole ridge had been torn violently from the main mountain mass of Walden's Ridge. During the eight years these entries were worked 1,140,000 bushels of excellent coal were taken out.

When the operations of the company on the south side of Rocky creek were arrested by the fault, a new opening was made on the northern side in the same outlying ridge, but bisected by Rocky creek. On the northern side of the creek this ridge does not extend further than one mile, and resembles a great irregular leaf attached by its stem to Walden's Ridge. Several seams of coal have been developed in this part of the ridge, with another in the bed of the creek below. The first one, near the top of the ridge, is about one foot thick, and shows good coal. The second, about eighty-three feet below, is about two feet thick. Forty-five feet below, and 173 feet above the level of the valley, a three-foot seam occurs. The coal from this seam shows some disturbance. It has a crumpled appearance, is highly lustrous, and gives out bituminous oil freely in burning. It is an excellent grate coal, and blacksmiths strongly recommend it for the fine welding heats that may be made with it. The seam at the opening dips gently to the northeast, but soon becomes horizontal. Overhead in the mine is a sandy shale, and the floor has two feet of fire-clay resting upon a gray shale. The seam of coal worked has a gray shale above, and a hard sand rock filled with fossil weeds, below.

The coal in Walden's Ridge, as exposed on the north side of the main branch of Rocky creek, is 2 feet 8 inches thick at the outcrop. This seam is 173 feet above the level of the bed of the stream, and corresponds to the seam the first above the new opening at the mines. Black shale four feet thick lies above, which makes a good hard roof. A grayish fire-clay of two or three feet thickness lies beneath the coal. Two seams are known to exist above this, but they have not been tested. All the seams are horizontal.

On the west side of Clemons creek, the southern prong of Rocky creek, there is a seam of coal $3\frac{1}{2}$ feet thick. This is lower than the one opened on Rocky creek by 100 feet, and may be a different seam from any mentioned or occurring in the outlying ridges.

In the bed of Rocky creek, about 500 yards above the point where the coal has been mined, there is a seam of varying thickness, from one to six feet, exposed on a level with the surface of the water. Lying upon the coal are five feet of black shale, with a thick bluff of sandstone above. The coal lies in a succession of pockets rather than in a continuous seam. The surface of the sandstone upon which it rests is filled with bowl-like cavities and trenches, all of which are filled with coal. The coal is also seen permeating the sandstone in dendritic veins.

The following section was taken by the aid of barometer on the north side of Rocky creek, and is approximately correct. Beginning at the top and going down the ridge we have:

Surface covered	85	feet.
Sandstone	40	"
Coal (a)	1	foot.
Shale	40	feet.
Sandstone	35	"
Black shale	8	"
Coal (b)	1.10	"
Fire-clay	8	"
Sandy shale	37	"
Coal (c)	2.6	"
Fire-clay	2	"
Gray shale	35 to 40 feet.	
Coal (d)	1 to 3 feet.	
Fire-clay	5	feet.
Sandstone	40	"
Gray shale	8	"
Coal (e)	4	"
Hard sandstone	70	"
Shale	1 to 6	"
Coal in pockets (f)	1 to 6	"
Sandstone with veins of coal.		

The section given above is rather a general section taken from several other sections. It represents about an average of all the sections.

Near the mine is a village of about 500 inhabitants, mostly Welch. It contains a school-house, church, store, post-office, two blacksmith shops and a carpenter shop.

The ridges between Tennessee river and the mountain at this place appear to have been swept away during the course of ages by the waters of Rocky and Sale creeks. A bottom covering some nine square miles has been thus formed. Its surface is generally rocky, especially near the base of the mountain; so much so, indeed, near the mountain, as to render it unsuitable for tillage. As the distance from the mountain increases the surface rocks disappear, until a very fair farming area is presented, and some very good farms are seen, though but a small proportion of the surface has been cleared. During the summer months the water in Rocky creek becomes very low, forming a succession of deep pools, joined together like necklaces by a trickling stream. The bed of the stream is exceedingly rough with water-worn bowlders. For water power, Sale creek and its tributaries are worthless.

Large ledges of limestone occur in the second parallel ridge from the mountain. The strata are all inclined to the north-west. The quality of the stone for making lime is good, but owing to the prevalence of seams and fissures it is not suitable for building purposes.

As to the iron ore of this region it may be mentioned that it often crops out in two or three seams on the sides of the outlying ridges, but in the valleys it is not met with, either because it lies below water level and becomes limestone, or because it is deeply covered by the overlying strata. Wherever it has been sought after, especially in the ridges, it has been found, though not always of such a quality or quantity as to justify working. The Dyestone strata along this line of road, with a few exceptions, are always found dipping at a high angle toward Walden's Ridge, as if the whole body of the Cumberland Table-land, by a downthrow, had bent the adjacent strata, making each cross section of the mountain and the first ridge like a sleigh-runner. A few deposits of brown hematite are found capping the hills, but not in sufficient abundance to justify the erection of furnaces.

From Sale Creek Mines to Smith's Cross Roads.

The distance from Sale Creek Mines to Smith's Cross Roads is nine miles, and the country between the two places presents some pleasing topographical features. Passing over Rocky creek going north-east, a high, bold, well-wooded ridge, called Black Oak ridge, rises on the east and continues in a line north-east without a gap for eight miles, and beyond Smith's Cross Roads, when it is cut in two by Richland creek. Sale creek comes out from Walden's Ridge two miles south of Smith's Cross Roads, and runs south-east until its course in that direction is checked by Black Oak ridge. It then turns south-west, and flows along the base of that ridge until it unites with Rocky creek near Sale Creek Mines. After this junction, it passes eastward through the wide gap already mentioned. Between the gorges formed in the mountain by Rocky creek and Sale creek is one made by McGill's creek, a tributary of Sale creek, and forms a union with that stream a short distance from the base of the mountain. In traveling up the line of railroad the gorge it makes is well marked in the side of the mountain, but the stream is not seen. Up this gorge some fine seams of coal are met with, one of which is four feet thick. This corresponds probably with coal (c) in the Rocky creek section. At least I judge so, from its elevation above the valley. This shows on the side of the mountain for a distance of thirty feet. The others, of which three are known to exist, are from one to three feet thick at the outcrops. This coal is convenient to the railroad, and so situated that tramways can be built from the railroad to the interior of the mountain at a cost not exceeding $5,000 per mile. The cost of opening the mines would be a mere trifle in comparison to the coal which could be reached. The seam is of uniform thickness as far as it has been prospected, and the tests applied to the coal show it to be of excellent quality for blacksmith and domestic purposes. The plateau of the mountain above shows a well wooded region, and a soil of more than average fertility for mountain lands. There is an immense growth of timber, consisting of chestnut, white and post oak, hickory, poplar, ash, and occasionally walnut. For colonization purposes the plateau above the coal would have a great value.

Cove creek gorge, just above, displays the same seams, as also the cut made by Sale creek, but they are not, at the outcrop, so thick as at Rocky creek.

Some excellent farming lands are seen in this section. Wide-spreading, level meadows and rich undulating fields are seen on both sides of the road. The St. Louis limestone, with its characteristic sinkholes, lies on the road, and supplies a strong, fertile soil. The timber upon this soil is very valuable. Large poplars, red oaks and white oaks are abundant, and will furnish a large amount of first-class lumber. In some of the bottoms below the St. Louis limestone the Nashville and Trenton rock appear.

At Smith's Cross Roads the ridge on the east forms a comparatively level plateau nearly two miles across, and the Tennessee river bottoms lie at its eastern base. The numerous river ridges below appear to have united to form one wide one at this place. The soil of this ridge is flinty, but productive. It is said to be well adapted to the growth of fruit. The surface immediately around Smith's Cross Roads is very level and beautiful. It is, indeed, a deeply-sunk basin, with high ridges and sharp hills bounding it on every side. On the west is Shin Bone Ridge, a flinty elevation from 200 to 300 feet above the valley that keeps its course parallel with the mountain. Between Shin Bone Ridge and the escarpment of Walden's Ridge is Lone Mountain, an isolated peak about two miles long at the base and one mile wide. It rises to the height of 780 feet above the valley, and reaches its highest elevation toward its northern end. Its southern extremity slopes gently down to Sale creek. A low, long spur, a ligament from its northern end, connects it with Walden's Ridge on the west. This spur or ligament forms the northern boundary of Cransmore's cove, Lone Mountain and a small Ridge hemming it on the east, and Sale creek and Walden's Ridge on the west. It is accessible only by going up Sale creek. This cove is from three to four miles long, and from three-fourths to one mile wide. The soil is good and the surface level, forming a fine agricultural area.

At the north-eastern extremity of Lone Mountain, Richland creek, a mountain torrent, breaks from Walden's Ridge, passing out in a south-eastern direction. Entering the gap made by this stream we find the strata of sandstone on the right going up dipping toward the mountain at an average angle of thirty degrees, but half a mile further up they become horizontal.

At this point Walden's Ridge attains an elevation of over 1,000 feet above the valley. On the opposite side of Richland creek its height is not so great by 150 feet. On the left bank of the creek, and right going up, seams of coal have been opened, the thickest of which is 3 feet 10 inches, but swells out to 6 feet 8 inches. This is one mile above the mouth of the gorge, and is the lowest seam, but the second seam shows about three feet of good coal, which may become thicker. This is the Rockwood seam. The fifth at this place has also been opened, and displays 21 inches of coal. The conglomerate appears here near the top of the mountain, 80 or 100 feet thick. Large blocks have tumbled down from above into the bed of Richland creek, greatly impeding the flow of the stream.

From the opening of the lower seam a tram road has been surveyed out to the valley, and a part of it graded, and some culverts made.

The character of the coal is variable. That taken from the second seam is spumous, fragile and shelly, and much resembles the Sewanee coal. It is very pure, and is doubtless a good coking coal. The entry in this seam has been driven in 200 yards, and shows a seam varying greatly in thickness, swelling out to several feet or more, and then squeezing down to fifteen inches. A dump platform has been constructed at the mouth of the entry. The tramway, as surveyed, is 140 feet below. The seam below this has been worked to a limited extent. An entry has been made into it thirty yards, and the coal taken therefrom was used in an old forge which was in operation before the war.

The slopes of Walden's Ridge are heavily timbered with chestnut oak, hickory, black oak and white oak. The sides of the mountain being very steep, wood can be brought by chutes from the top of the mountain to the valley below.

One mile above, from the mouth of Richland creek gorge, several tributary streams enter Richland creek, swelling its volume and increasing its value. Each one of these streams have made cross ravines in the gulf of Richland creek, laying bare the coal beds. It would be no difficult task to construct railroad lines up each of these cross ravines, and so multiply the coal product indefinitely.

On Morgan's turnpike, just as the road begins to ascend the mountain, is a large curled mass of coal. It is very much crushed, and doubtless rolled down from above. It burns well, but the quantity is uncertain. Two or three seams are seen in ascending the mountain by this road.

I have spoken of Cransmore's cove. Near the head of this, but on the western side, a coal bed showing a thickness of thirty inches has been opened and worked for local purposes. The coal is lustrous and beautiful, and is said to burn freely. This seam, as measured by the barometer, is 33 feet lower than the second mentioned as occurring on Richland creek. The coal at this place would be difficult, if not impossible, to work from the present entry, as the strata all dip back into the mountain as much as three inches to the yard. Bluish, sandy and buff-colored shales 20 feet thick overlie the coal with a floor of hard black shale three feet thick, which rests upon a great thickness of sandstone.

From the head of Cransmore cove a stream of water plunges over a precipice 75 feet high. The thickness of the sandstone forming the bluff at this point is 100 feet or more. The view from the head of the cove is extensive, varied, and beautiful.

Passing now to a consideration of the beds of iron ore in the region around Smith's Cross Roads, we find both the fossil ores and the brown hematite in considerable abundance. Directly east of the point where Richland creek leaves the mountain, the dyestone ore is found in Shin Bone ridge outcropping on its western slope, and dipping as usual to the north-west. The ridge containing it is low as compared with the Dyestone ridges at other places. There is also an absence of the white oak mountain sandstone which, wherever it prevails, is mountain-making in its character. The fossil ore, as it occurs in this locality, is interstratified with beds of grayish slate. The first point examined had a thickness of only nine inches, which was well exposed by a drift which had been run into the hill for fifteen or twenty yards. The seam shows great contortions and numerous plications rising up in short folds, wrinkled like the folds of a great curtain, having a general dip, however, of about

70 degrees. The line of strike runs about north 20 degrees, east about parallel with the general course of Walden's Ridge.

A ditch a hundred yards further north has been dug on the face of the hill across the line of strike, which reveals six or more thin seams of fossil ore, with grayish shale between. All the seams occur within the distance of 37 feet measured on the slope of the hill. The following section, measured perpendicular to the direction of the strata, will give a correct idea of the ore as it occurs at this place. Beginning with the lowest, but highest on the hill, we have:

Ore...	3 inches.
Gray shale...	4 feet.
Ore...	4 inches.
Shale...	12 inches.
Ore...	3 inches.
Shale...	11 inches.
Ore...	6 inches.
Shale...	10 feet.
Ore...	6 inches.
Shale...	8 feet.
Ore...	7 inches.
Shale of great thickness.	

This lead of ore is traceable by its outcrop for three miles up the valley. It is very hard, and contains a sensible quantity of calcite and siliceous material. It has a dull, dead color, with adhering siliceous scales, and but few perceptible fossils, these being confined to a few crinoidal buttons.

Upon the Morgan turnpike a curled mass of coal has been mentioned. Just below this, about 100 yards, is a bed of blue siliceous shale, which makes excellent whetstones. Half way to the top of the mountain a bed of brown hematite occurs. About fifteen or twenty tons have been taken out. It occurs regularly stratified. It is of a poor quality, being very siliceous. I do not think the deposit of any great value.

Near the top of the mountain, and lying on both sides of the road, a white sandstone is found, from which grindstones of good grit have been manufactured. It is soft, and wears easily.

Lere Mountain has been spoken of. It is a high sandstone ridge, covered, for the most part, with a heavy growth of black oak, pine and chestnut oak. From its eastern side it is cut by two gorges, nearly severing the mountain into three parts. In the most southern of these gorges is a considerable deposit of brown hematite of good quality. It covers the surface of the ground on the side of the gorge for several hundred feet, and in a tongue of land that lies in the bottom of the ravine it sticks out in blocks weighing several tons. From the tests given it is of first rate quality, yielding about fifty per cent. of metallic iron. It occurs in compact masses. It is impossible to say how extensive the deposit is, or whether it will afford a sufficient amount to justify the erection of a furnace without more extensive prospecting. Its position is easily reached, and it can be carried down a gentle slope to the railroad, a mile distant. Brown hematite is also found in portions of Shin Bone ridge, near its crest, as also in many other ridges and hills in the neighborhood.

In the valley a bog ore is found underlying the meadows to such an extent as to interfere with the proper cultivation of the soil. It is at places several feet thick.

An English company has bought 40,000 acres of mineral and agricultural lands in the vicinity of this place. This company has made 1,700,000 bricks, with which to erect two furnaces at or near Smith's Cross Roads, and one rolling mill. The progress of this enterprise has been impeded by the depression of the iron interests.

Smith's Cross Roads is a small village in Rhea county,

of 100 inhabitants, and contains one academy, three stores, one blacksmith shop, one boot and shoe shop, one wagon making and one saddler's shop.

FROM SMITH'S CROSS ROADS TO RHEA SPRINGS.

The Tennessee Valley narrows just above Smith's Cross Roads, but widens out into a beautiful expanse a mile or two above. The surface at intervals swells into gentle hills, with wide fertile lowlands between. Little Richland creek, a confluent of Big Richland, rises nine miles north of Smith's Cross Roads, and by many a convolution winds beside the fertile pastures, and adds beauty and attractiveness to the pastoral scene. It gathers in its course, from numerous springs, water enough to drive grist mills. Better farms and better farm houses appear in this section than in those heretofore spoken of. An air of thrift is everywhere seen, and the farms are well stocked with every thing necessary to insure success in their calling.

Shin Bone ridge skirts the mountain with a few low gaps, which give access to Back Valley. It is more subdued here than below, and some of its slopes have been brought into cultivation. Back Valley, lying between this and the mountain, is very narrow and trough-like.

On the eastern side of the Tennessee Valley, Valley ridge, a continuation of Black Oak ridge, sinks to a lower level, and is flattened out. The soil is flinty and unproductive, and the timber upon it is not so heavy as below Smith's Cross Roads, though there are some farms upon it. It is excellent for fruits and wheat. Corn yields only about ten or fifteen bushels per acre. Three miles above Smith's Cross Roads, on the eastern side of the mountain, a good bank of coal has been opened and worked for local purposes. It is known as Stewart's bank. The seam is three feet thick, and the coal is of excellent quality. In Read's gulf, four miles higher up, two good seams of coal lie exposed. Brown hematite is found along the slopes of Valley ridge, but not in any great quantity.

In this part of Tennessee Valley the crops yield, in good seasons, about as follows:

Hay, from herds grass mainly..........	1 to 1½ tons per acre.	
Corn...	30 to 35 bushels per acre.	
Wheat...	10 " "
Oats...	25 to 30 " "
Sorghum...	100 gallons "

With careful preparation of the soil, as much as forty bushels of wheat have been grown per acre. This is done upon clover sod. For the growth of clover the lands of the valley are well suited, having a large proportion of clay and carbonate of lime in their composition. Tobacco also grows well upon the slopes of the hills, and sometimes makes an average return of 800 pounds per acre. Much of the soil of this section could be made profitable by growing this staple. A fine silky article can be made here which would bring a high price from the manufacturer.

The rearing of stock is not carried on so extensively as might be in this section. The mountain lands would furnish a large amount of highway pasturage, while winter supplies could be grown cheaply in the valley. Those who have engaged in this branch of husbandry find it very profitable for the time and labor expended.

Sedge grass is very troublesome in the valleys, and destroys meadows in a few years. Its extirpation would add greatly to the value of the lands. The soil of the valley, as before stated, is, principally, a calcareous loam, but there are strips lying on the borders of Little Richland which are water-soaked. The land has a whitish color, and while it grows herds grass luxuriantly, is not well suited for the production of other crops. The average width of the bottom is three-fourths of a mile. The timber, though not so large or abundant as in the section embraced between

Sale Creek Mines and Smith's Cross Roads, is essentially of the same kinds. Poplar, oak and pine predominate. Lumber sells for $12.50 per thousand, except walnut, which is worth $30 per thousand, and scarce.

This region is well watered by springs which break out from Valley ridge and from the mountain. Limestone, freestone and chalybeate waters are often found within a short distance of each other.

It may be mentioned that the mountain lying on the west of the railroad in this section is settling up rapidly by persons who propose to make fruit-raising a specialty. Grapes, peaches, plums and apples are all said to do well, and a large planting has been made of these during the past two years. As soon as the building of the railroad became an assured fact, the planting of orchards began, and I was assured that thousands of acres would be in bearing in a few years on this section, and within four miles of the railroad. A large amount of land will also be devoted to the growing of onions and Irish potatoes. Wild grapes grow profusely upon the top of the mountain, and ripen in such abundance as to make them an article of traffic. The farming lands of the valley are worth from twenty to forty dollars per acre; on the valley ridges, from three to ten; on the mountain, from one to five; the first figures in each case representing unimproved lands, and the second improved. The farmers in the valley usually have their timber supplies on the ridges.

Labor is said to be abundant, but of poor quality, and not trustworthy. In the valley from ten to twelve dollars per month and board are paid. Schools have been sadly neglected. In many localities of this section there are no schools of any sort. From Little Richland Station (No. 213) up to Clear creek the valley is much like that below, only not so wide. Clear creek breaks out from Walden's Ridge about forty-seven miles above Chattanooga. It supplies some tolerably good water powers. In the chasm formed by this stream four good seams of coal may be seen, the thickest of which is said to be six feet, but I did not see it. Above Clear creek, and between it and Piney, which is three miles above, the spurs from Shin Bone ridge shoot out into the valley, forming a succession of swelling tongues, with gentle slopes. Much of the farming lands here have been badly worn. Red hills and gullies disfigure the farms. The mountain escarpment between the two last named streams is about 500 feet high, but back a mile or more it rises 300 feet higher, forming a beautiful table-land upon the higher plane.

On Piney four seams of coal are also seen, and judging from their respective elevations, I take them to be identical with those at Clear creek, thus forming between the two streams a splendid coal field, which could be worked on three sides. The thickness of the upper seam is four feet of good block coal. Two hundred feet below is a seam three feet thick, corresponding with the Rockwood seam. The coal in this is soft and easily crushed. The Valley ridge opposite this coal area flattens down into a broad flat plain, which extends eastward seven miles to the Tennessee river. Through this plateau land Piney flows on its way to the Tennessee river. Spurs run from the north and south, and cramp in the plateau at a few places to less than half a mile; at other places the distance between the heads of the spurs is from three to four miles.

RHEA SPRINGS.

These springs are situated about the centre of this flattened area, near the banks of Piney. For many years these springs have been a favorite resort during the summer months. The water is alkaline, though called sulphur, the principal ingredients being sulphate of lime, sulphate

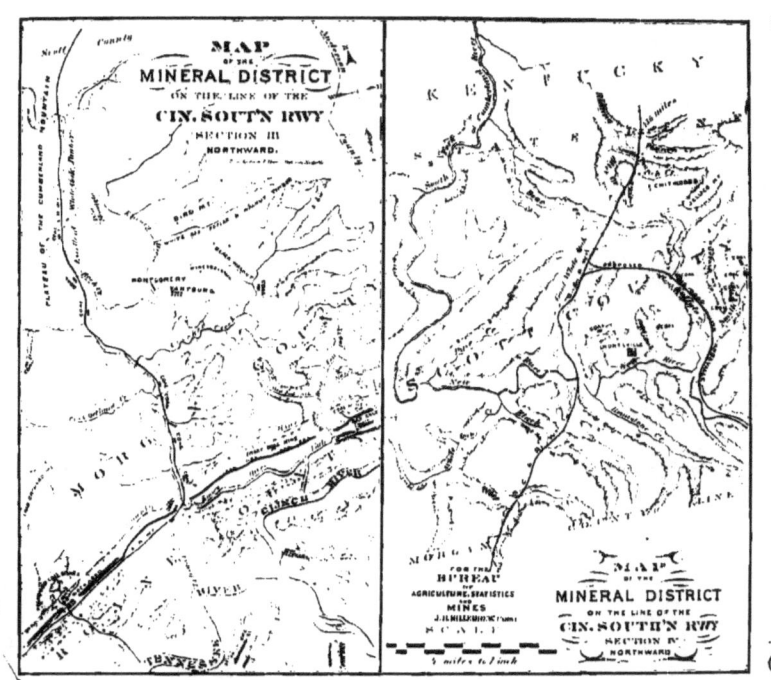

of magnesia, sulphate of soda, silicate of soda, with a little salt. The water is said to have a healthy effect upon the stomach and bowels. It is shipped to nearly every State in the Union. A small village has sprung up at the springs, and presents quite a neat and tasteful appearance. Beautiful shade trees embower every cottage, and the green grass covers the surface of the ground, giving a pleasing and attractive appearance to the surroundings. Piney, which flows through the village, is bountifully supplied with fish, the principal species being the black bass, red horse, perch, drum, cat fish, buffalo, jack, and river salmon. On the mountains and ridges game is abundant. Deer, wild turkeys, squirrels, hares and partridges are numerous. Occasionally a bear or wild cat is met with.

The population of Rhea Springs is about 400. There are in the place four stores, one drug store, two blacksmith shops, one wagon shop, three boot and shoe establishments, two harness shops, one tin shop, one flouring mill, one photograph gallery, one cabinet-maker's shop, three churches, one livery stable, one masonic lodge, and one hotel capable of accommodating 125 persons.

From Rhea Springs to Rockwood.

The few short, broken ridges north of Rhea Springs soon give way to an undulating valley which spreads out quite a half mile wide. This valley lies east of the Tennessee Valley, along which the railroad passes, with one intervening ridge. Another ridge lies between this valley and the Tennessee river. Passing from Rhea Springs in a northwesterly direction, across a low ridge to the railroad, or Tennessee Valley, we find some excellent farming lands, the valley being very wide and productive. Shin Bone Ridge here runs very near the mountain. At a point about nine miles below Rockwood this ridge has a wide gap, and sandstone ledges are found in the Tennessee Valley, a very rare occurrence. In these sandstone ledges masses of crushed coal are met with. This coal occurs on the farm of David Roddy. The valley narrows near White's creek. This stream has a confined valley, and like the others, makes a deep cut in the mountain. Its point of exit from the mountain is six miles below Rockwood. North of this stream the valley is almost shut out by the approaching ridges, leaving only an elevated trough through which the railroad passes. From White's creek to Rockwood the ridges run in and nearly fill up the valley. Sometimes the valley is made up of a few level areas lying between the broken ridges. These little valleys take every form, the spurs coming down from every direction like the points of a star. Clumps of dark, thick forests are scattered at intervals, with small patches of cleared land. Turnpike creek, which rises above Rockwood, winds its course around the numerous spurs and along fruitful basins. West of this stream the dyestone ore appears, dipping toward the mountain in a continuous seam, nowhere broken. The cherty ridges of the Knox group appear on the east, and the black shale and mountain limestone on the west. Near the mouth of White's creek two forges are in operation which make each, when in blast, about 200 pounds of bar iron per day. The ore is the dyestone obtained from the face of the ridge near the mountain. One ton of ore makes 700 pounds of bar iron. One hundred bushels of charcoal make 200 pounds of iron. The hammerer and tender are paid 20 per cent. of the iron made.

The coal up White's creek is abundant. On a little stream, Piney by name, that enters White's creek from the north, is an outcrop exposed by erosion of the water, which is four feet thick. The coal appears in the main mountain mass, and is probably the same as the Rockwood seam. Two other seams are found in White's creek gap, one of which is three feet four inches thick, and the second about three feet. The last is the lowest. The coal from this is soft and spongy. The coal from the other two mentioned appears to be good. That on Piney is a close, compact, block coal, and said to be the best welding coal that has been found on the mountain.

ROCKWOOD.

As an industrial enterprise, no place in the State deserves more notice than Rockwood. It is situated in Roane county, at the foot of the Cumberland Mountain, four miles from the Tennessee river, and seventy-two miles above Chattanooga. It has a population of 1200. Ten years ago the place where this village now stands was a wilderness. By the persistent energy of General J. T. Wilder, W. P. Rathburn and others, a company with a capital of $1,000,000 was formed, and two blast furnaces erected, designated as Rockwood No. 1 and Rockwood No. 2. No. 1 is 42 feet high, closed top, with bell and hopper, hot blast, 3 tuyers of $4\frac{1}{2}$ inches each; capacity per day, 25 tons. No. 2 is 65 feet high, closed top, bosh 16 feet, hot blast, 4 tuyers; capacity, 40 tons per day. Boilers are heated by gas brought down from top of furnace by a downcomer, made of 3-16 iron plate, and lined with fire brick. There are two engines, which are run alternately a week at a time. No. 1 engine has an air cylinder 6 feet in diameter, with 4 feet stroke. No 2 has a cylinder 7 feet in diameter, with 4 feet stroke. No. 1. makes 22 revolutions, and No. 2 18 revolutions per minute. Rockwood No. 1 was in blast at the time of my visit in October. The charges were as follows, thirty being made in 24 hours:

Coal	580 lbs.
Coke	2,046 "
Limestone	660 "
Ore, from Company's lands	1,550 "
Ore, from Kindricks, across Tennessee River	1,550 "

With these charges an average of 18½ tons of pig iron were made daily. The ore used is the fossil red hematite or dyestone, one-half of which is obtained from the Company's land, and the other half from near the head of Half Moon Island, across the river nine miles south of Rockwood. This ore is mined and put on the Company's cars at Rockwood landing, four miles from the furnace, at $2 per ton. The ore goes raw in the furnace without any previous calcination. The amount of iron made at Rockwood from September 1, 1875, to August 31, 1876, is as follows:

September, 1875	484	tons.
October, "	530	"
November, "	550	"
December, "	546½	"
January, 1876	507	"
February, "	516	"
March, "	565½	"
April, "	550	"
May, "	533	"
June, "	528½	"
July, "	468	"
August, "	511	"

The iron is classed mostly mill No. 2, though foundry is made when required. The whole product is consumed by the rolling mill at Chattanooga, belonging to the same company.

The coal mines at Rockwood furnish an interesting study. The strata are greatly disturbed, and the coal is found rolled up in great masses, often from forty to one hundred feet thick. The point of attack is in the gorge cut by Turnpike creek. The surface of the mountain at this point shows a gentle sag, while the seam of coal dips in opposite directions to the contour of the surface.

The axis of the anticlinal runs about north 20 degrees east. Three main entries or levels have been driven into the coal seam at this place, designated as Nos. 1, 2 & 3.

No. 1, which is the lowest, and last one made, enters by a cross cut through the underlying sandstone for 500 feet before the coal seam is met with. Here it is two feet thick. One foot of fire clay underlies it, and just above is an inch of soft, putty-like clay, which continues even where the coal is pinched out, and serves as a guide in running drifts where there is no coal. The persistency of this soft clay is remarkable, and is peculiar, as far as my observations extend, to the coal at Rockwood. Above this clay is a very hard, black, calcareous shale. The coal seam here shows a dip upward of 32 degrees. The entry is made through a very hard sandstone, upon which common blasting powder has but little effect. It was found necessary to use dynamite.

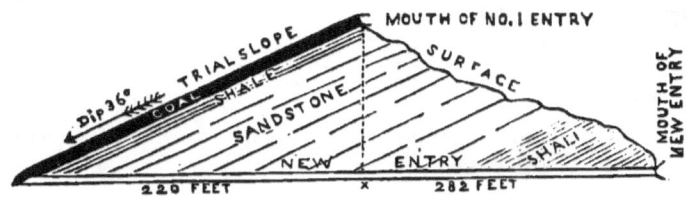

Section at Rockwood.

The coal from this entry is very hard, closely resembling an anthracite in appearance. It also appears to be freer from shale than that taken from the other levels. The seam worked upward has increased to six feet.

Level No. 2 (called New Bank), is 150 feet above the last. At this the strata was followed down 200 feet, with only two degrees variation. This second entry is nearly a mile in length, and runs around on two sides of a synclinal fold, forming a basin, or spoon-like depression between the two sides of the entry, which lies several hundred feet below. The axis of this synclinal, like that of the anticlinal referred to, runs north 20 degrees east. A better idea can be obtained of this entry by an inspection of the diagram below. The arrows show the dip of the coal.

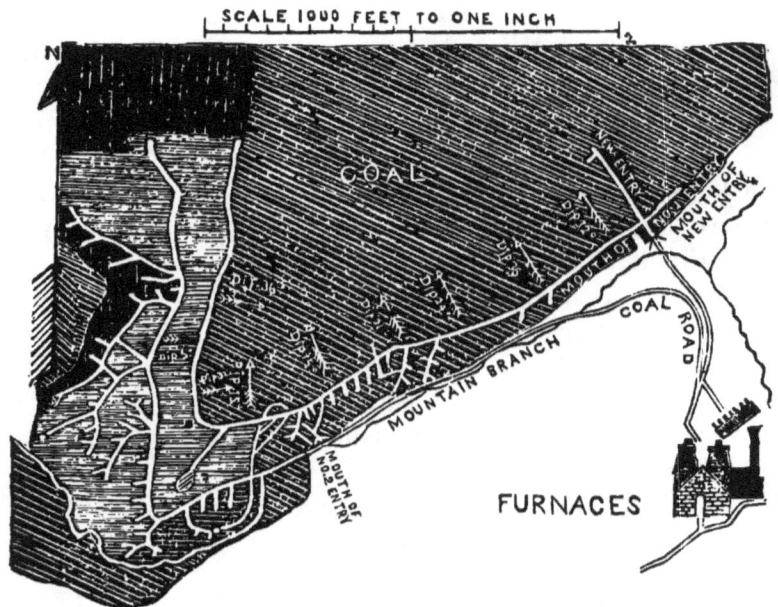

Underground Plan of the Roane Iron Company's Coal Mines, Rockwood, Roane county, Tennessee.

The seam of coal, as developed by the working in this entry, is very wavy and irregular, exhibiting numerous plications or folds. Sometimes within a few hundred yards the thickness of the coal may vary twenty feet. Great rolls occur like huge waves, which may thin down to a mere wafer. The lamination shows great disturbance, appearing sometimes in a succession of wrinkles, again in concentric, shelly masses. The coal is not homogeneous. Some of it is very hard, other specimens are soft, and crumble to the touch. Lenticular particles of shale are often found penetrating the mass as though it had been ground up and mingled with the coal. At other places the shale is absent and the coal very pure. When the roof is shelly and tender, and filled with seams, more or less shale is found intermixed with the coal. Usually the roof of this entry is composed of a hard, dark-colored calcareous shale, which crumbles by exposure. As this entry has been driven in nearly on a water-level, the roof, by reason of the dip of the strata, is inclined overhead like the roof of a shed.

A third level or entry, from which a large amount of coal has been taken, is still higher up the mountain. The coal in this sometimes attains, by reason of the folds, an extraordinary thickness. At one place the thickness, measured perpendicular to the plane of the horizon, is 110 feet. This occurs near the outcrop in the bed of the stream above the mouth of the entry.

A new drift is being made with the strata, to connect the second level with the third. By this the coal can be brought down so as to save quite half a mile of tram-road on the outside, and by which the coal can be taken out more economically. A new tramway has been constructed leading from the mouth of level No. 1 to a point just above the coke ovens. The coal here is received into a double chute, the lump coal above and fine coal below. The coal will be shot into cars instead of carts, as heretofore, and a track laid over the ovens will permit the introduction of larger quantities of coal into them at once—two car loads making an ovenfull, in place of eight cart loads as heretofore. Only one seam of importance has been found at this place. Some smaller ones appear, but they have never been tested sufficiently to form a correct idea as to their value. If it be true, as is supposed, that the Rockwood seam is the equivalent of the Sewanee, and of No. 6 at the Emory mines higher up, there ought to be several valuable seams below, which can only be ascertained by deep boring. The unusual disturbance everywhere visible in the strata at Rockwood, may have thrown the lower seams below the level of the valley. According to the section taken by Prof. Bradley at Emory mines, the next lower seam should be at least 220 feet below the main Rockwood, excluding, of course, the small seam seen near the mouth of level No.

1. This small seam doubtless is the same which appears in the Sewanee section, as lying 42 feet below the main Sewanee. The quantity of coal mined at this place and used in the furnaces from September 1, 1875, to August 31, 1876, inclusive, is shown in the subjoined table:

September, 1875	56,944	bushels.
October, "	44,441	"
November, "	61,796	"
December, "	54,079	"
January, 1876	40,149	"
February, "	45,312	"
March, "	54,666	"
April, "	63,103	"
May, "	48,834	"
June, "	51,406	"
July, "	42,794	"
August, "	47,141	"
Aggregating for the year	610,665	bushels.

About six-sevenths of this quantity is converted into coke, one-seventh being used raw in the furnace. The coal yields about 59 per cent. of coke, which, though sometimes injured by the presence of shaly matter, has proved quite good enough for all furnace purposes. Twenty-eight coke ovens are kept in blast, with a capacity each of 130 bushels.

The iron ore for the furnace is obtained from a ridge, or rather series of long, rounded hills, lying on the southeastern side of the valley in which the furnace is situated. The seam here is broken by numerous faults, forming a broken line. The seam may continue perfectly straight for a hundred yards or more, when it ends abruptly in a shaly bank, but it is always found to the right or left a few yards distant, without a trace intervening; again, forming on the outcrop a curved line like the letter S. The thickness of the seam at this place will average about four feet, besides four inches of ferruginous limestone below, which adheres to a dark-colored shale. Beautiful specimens of brown hematite, in "pots" and in laminated masses, are forming above the stratified dyestone, by the infiltration of water through the shales. The seam of ore is highly inclined towards the mountain; indeed, in places it is almost perpendicular to the horizon. Numerous small folds occur, making a congeries of small, wavy layers, only a few inches across, showing intense lateral pressure. A section was taken above the furnace as follows, beginning at the top:

Siliceous group of the Lower Carboniferous.
Black shale, about.. 75 feet.
Gray shale .... 22 "
Hard, bluish shale .... 1 "
Dyestone ore... 4 "
Calcareous dyestone... 4 inches.
Bluish and green shales, about................................ 60 feet.
Reddish calcareous shales, alternating with ledges
of limestone, weathering badly.......................... 100 "

Beneath the last mentioned strata the Trenton rocks crop out in the valley, nearly on edge, and of great thickness. Beyond the valley the Knox limestones appear, a fault occurring here.

The seam at Rockwood has been worked to the water level for about four miles. The four inches of calcareous dyestone lying below is not received at the furnace. The ore from the company's lands costs, delivered at the furnace, $1.40 per ton; that from other points, $2. The ore, as it appears in the seam three miles above Rockwood, is very superior, being oolitic, and resembling the specular ore. It is made up of small flattened or rounded grains. It is very soft, and has a steely appearance. Where the oolitic ore is found, the seam is often disturbed by plications or "horsebacks." By exposure this ore soon crumbles into a powdery mass. It is the richest ore found around the furnace. The analyses below, made by A. W. Kinsey, chemist, will give the relative value of the different varieties. For these analyses I am indebted to C. Constable, the energetic and intelligent manager of the furnaces:

No. 1. Fine ore, soft, steely; separated from the lump.

Peroxide of iron	71.64
Lime and alumina	14.56
Silica	8.80
Phosphorus	.72
Metallic iron	50 15

No. 2. Lump, dull ore, soft; constituting the average run of ore.

Peroxide of iron	67.29
Lime and alumina	11.20
Silica	8.00
Phosphorus	.67
Metallic iron	47.10

No. 3. Fine, steely, hard ore.

Peroxide of iron	64.43
Lime	14.00
Silica	7.80
Phosphorus	.61
Metallic iron	45.10

No. 4. Ore from Kindrick's bank across the river, and washed at the furnace. A soft, dark-colored, porous ore; after crumbling, resembling a reddish, loamy soil. Analyses by Kenneth Robertson.

Peroxide of iron	73.96
Alumina	8.04
Lime	1.09
Silica	9.53
Phosphorus	.49
Water, carbonic acid, etc	5.00
Metallic iron	51.77

No. 5. Another sample from same place.

Peroxide of iron	75.00
Alumina	6.81
Lime	.00
Silica	13.00
Phosphorus	.59
Water, carbonic acid, etc	4.60
Metallic iron	52.50

The coal worked in the furnace, average run of the mines, shows the following by analysis:

Carbon	76.40
Volatile matter	16.50
Ash	6.65
Sulphur	.33
Loss	.18

The shale which is sometimes found immediately associated with the coal, and always lying above and forming the roof, shows the following ingredients:

Peroxide of iron	6.47
Alumina	22.33
Lime	5.05
Silica	62.66

The wages paid, and the men employed, at the furnace are as follows:

One founder, $125 per month.
Two keepers, each $1.75 per day and an interest of one cent per ton on all metal made.
Two helpers, at $1.50 each.
Six fillers—top fillers, per day, $1.50; bottom, $1.25.
One limestone breaker, per day, $1.
Two engineers, each, per day, $2.
Common laborers, per day, $1.
One oiler, per day, 75 cents.
Fireman in mines, per month, $100.
One watchman, per day, $1.25.
Four inside drivers, each, per day, $1.45.
Five outside drivers, each, per day, $1.30.
Two iron men, each, per day, $1.25.
Twenty miners are employed in the mines, who are paid two cents per bushel for raising coal.
Nine men and one foreman are employed in the coke yard. The foreman receives $60 per month, and oven-tenders 50 cents per oven. Three drivers are also employed, at $1 per day.

For the purpose of conveying the iron from the furnace to the river, a narrow-gauge railroad has been constructed to Rockwood landing at King's creek, five miles distant.

An engine of the capacity of ten tons is used on the road. This capacity will be increased to fifteen tons by an improvement in the grade of the road.

The effects upon the surrounding country by the construction of these furnaces are everywhere apparent. Neat farm houses have sprung up, and a lively demand has been created for all farm products. The village has three churches, two public schools, one store, one hotel, six blacksmith shops, two wagon shops, one livery stable, one bakery, one tin shop, and three shoemakers' shops. All this improvement has taken place in the last eight years, and shows in the most practical manner the effects of manufactures upon the agricultural interests of the State. Wages have been advanced in price, but agricultural products have advanced at a greater ratio. Civilization, with all its ameliorating influences, has sprung up in a spot that was a wilderness ten years ago. Lands are more valuable, and a general air of prosperity pervades the whole region.

From Rockwood to Emory Mine.

The valley, as it extends above Rockwood, continues broken, but the amount of arable land is greater than the section below from White's creek to Rockwood, and more fertile. The average yield of wheat is 10 bushels per acre; corn, 40; oats, 35. The valley terminates at Keagan's tunnel, near Emory gap, a spur running from the mountain to the ridges on the east.

Patches of the Trenton rocks are seen at places cropping out at the surface. The Clinton or dyestone formation is continuous, and forms quite an interesting study at the Emory Gap tunnel, seven miles above. At this place a fault occurs, the downthrow of the Cumberland Table-land on the west, and the uplift of the Knox group on the east, throwing all the strata of the Dyestone group entirely over, reversing the order not only in dip but in position. The strata here dip south-east at an angle of 32 degrees. Usually the Dyestone group dips under the mountain. The edge of the strata coming out from the mountain has been folded back, throwing the black shale and Siliceous group below the iron ore. The section taken at Emory mine, by Professor Bradley, (see Emory Mines) illustrates the manner of this folding back.

The tunnel crosses the strata at an angle S. 60° W., and a section, on next page, kindly furnished me by C. Breckinridge, division engineer, will prove an interesting study for geologists.

From the Emory Gap or Keagan Tunnel, eastward to Kingston, rounded, cherty ridges prevail, with trough-like ravines. The ridge nearest the railroad has a comparatively flat top, with some cultivated areas, though the soil is thin. The prevailing timber is black oak, white oak and pine, with an undergrowth of dogwood. Judging from the character of the natural growth, the soil is well adapted to the growth of tobacco. The ridge nearest the Tennessee River, and running parallel with it, is about 200 feet high, well wooded, and belongs to the Knox formation.

Kingston is situated at the junction of the Clinch and Tennessee Rivers, on the eastern side of the former, and north of the latter stream. It is 120 miles by river from Chattanooga, and five miles from the Cincinnati Southern Railroad. It has a population of about 1000, and is well situated for manufacturing establishments. It has eight or ten commercial establishments. An establishment for the manufacture of steel has been recently erected. The steel is made by a new process, and takes a high rank in the market for the manufacture of tools. Only six hands are employed, and the product amounts to about 26,000 lbs. per month.

A large amount of freight is brought down the Clinch

EMORY GAP TUNNEL, CINCINNATI SOUTHERN RAILWAY.

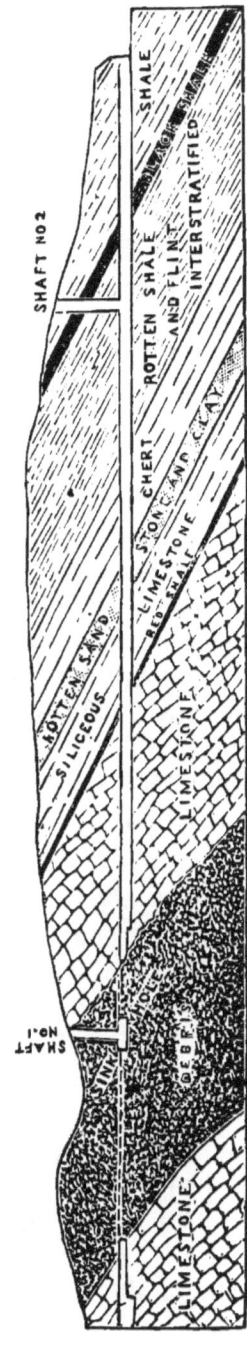

Vertical Section.

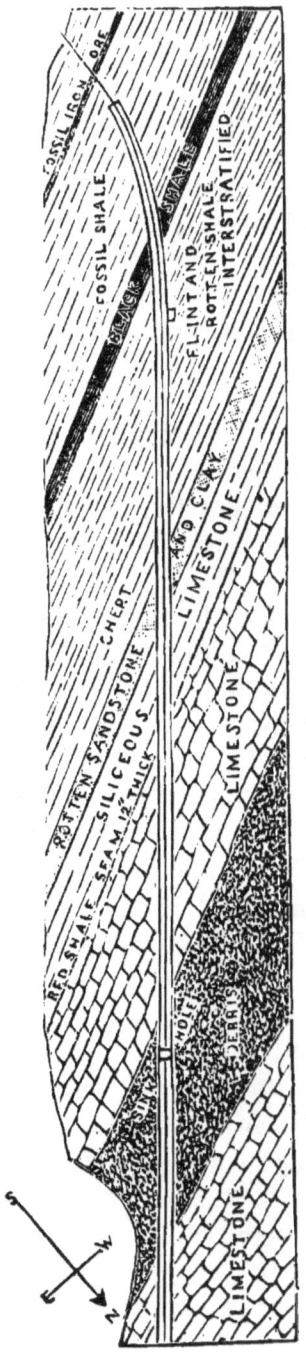

Horizontal Section.

during high water. It is estimated that 250 flat boats annually come down that stream, loaded with corn, bacon, hay, oats, dried fruits, pig-iron from Cumberland Gap, and coal from Emory mine, Poplar Gap, and points above. Seven steamboats ply the Tennessee River to this point and below. Over 100 rafts of saw-logs, in addition to other produce, are floated to Chattanooga and points below from the country watered by the Clinch. Immediately in the vicinity of Kingston there are extensive and valuable deposits of iron ore. Those south of the river have been mentioned in the report of the Ococe and Hiwassee mineral district. Deposits of brown hematite are found in a ridge east of Kingston. Baryta occurs, of excellent quality, near the Tennessee River. Some beautiful variegated marble is found south of the same stream. Coal exists in great abundance within six miles of the town, and many valuable forests of excellent timber surround it. The coal can be brought down the Clinch river from the Emory mine, Oakdale, Poplar Creek, Coal Creek, and from other points, at a small cost. Slack-water navigation would enable the coal to be brought out at any season. For the manufacture of charcoal and stone-coal iron there are but few places that combine so many natural advantages as Kingston. Should the proposed line of railroad, leading from Lenoir's, on the East Tennessee, Virginia and Georgia Railroad, to Emory Gap, on the Cincinnati Southern, be constructed, Kingston would soon rival in wealth and population any place in East Tennessee. The farming lands surrounding it are excellent, and supplies could be raised to feed a large population. The first and second bottoms, which include all the lands between the rivers and the hills, are half a mile, and sometimes even a mile wide. It rarely happens that good bottom lands are found on opposite sides of this stream, but this happens below Kingston. The lower bottoms, with slovenly cultivation, make from fifty to sixty bushels of corn per acre, and hay in great quantities. Oats frequently fail by reason of rust on the lower lands, which yield from fifteen to twenty bushels on clover sod. Board timber is abundant, and lumber of all kinds is cheap, varying, according to quality, from one dollar to one dollar and fifty cents per hundred.

Emory Coal Mines.

These mines have been opened on the south-eastern side of Walden's Ridge, along the north-eastern line of Roane county, between the Little Emory and Big Emory rivers, and two or three miles distant from the railroad.

There are two thick seams of coal at this place, besides three or four thin ones. The main seam worked is in Walden's Ridge, and is the equivalent of the Rockwood seam, and designated in Prof. Bradley's section as Coal No. 6. Its average thickness is about four feet, while in many places it reaches five, though pinching down at others to three or less. The average dip is about sixty degrees. The section taken from Prof. Bradley's report to the Wilcox Mining Company, given below, will show the general position of the strata:

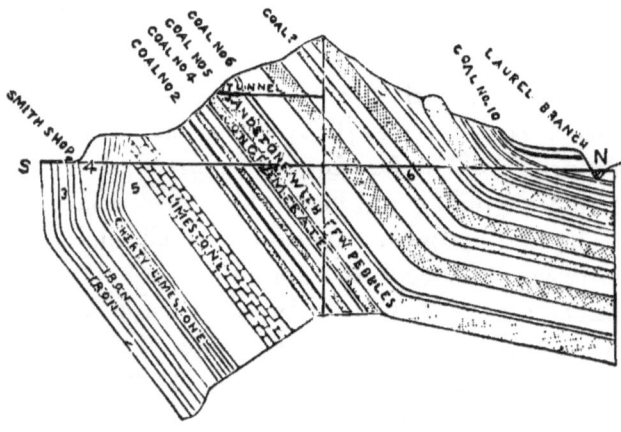

If this section were continued southward to the dump-house on Big Emory river, it would pass across about 3,000 feet of Cincinnati and Trenton rocks and another band of the Dyestone group. East of the dump-house the Black Slate and St. Louis limestones are seen. The position of the strata 1,200 yards east of Bemess ferry on Big Emory north to Whetstone mountain, is so interesting, that I give Prof. Bradley's description in full, he having spent a considerable time upon the ground in working it out.

"In approaching the property," says Prof. Bradley in his able and elaborate report, "whether by the direct road from Knoxville or from Kingston, and while yet about two miles from the Company's store, we pass from the Knox group across the fault"—(the fault spoken of begins near Bemess ferry and runs east, showing on the south the shales of the Knox group, and on the north the Dyestone group)—"just mentioned, directly to the shales of the Dyestone group, dipping southward. At the tannery, on the Knoxville road, one bed of the dyestone or argillaceous lenticular iron ore is exposed; and the second may exist, though I have not seen it here. Thence we cross an anticlinal valley, in which the Cincinnati group limestones are not generally uncovered by the overlying shales, except near the Big Emory, and find it followed by a synclinal ridge, at the nearer base of which both bands of dyestone are developed, and have been worked, in former years, for the supply of the old Emory furnace, long since destroyed, whose site is recognized by the masses of cinders scattered on the left of the road as we approach the ford of little Emory river. Both the Black Shale and the Subcarboniferous limestones are here prominently developed; and the section at this point afforded the larger measures of thickness of these beds recorded in the general section. The synclinal fold is a very sharp one, the dip on its southern side being here 84° (N. 30° W.), while on its northern side it reaches 63°

and 66° (S. 30° E.). Where it approaches the Big Emory, the ridge has been so cut off by ancient river action as to put the outcrops of the iron seams, on its southern side, out of sight under the alluvium; at the same time, the northern side of the fold has become so nearly vertical as to leave it doubtful which way the beds dip, without more excavation than has yet been done. The synclinal has not been traced across and beyond the bed of the river: but the iron seams on its northern side are exposed where they cross the valley road, about two miles further west."

The structure will be best understood by constant reference to the accompanying section, as given by Prof. Bradley.

"Crossing the anticlinal of the valley, the axis of which runs near the Company's store, we approach Walden's Ridge. The iron ore said to have been encountered in digging the cellar of Mr. D'Armond's new house, has not been found at any other point; and we can only infer that it is a local development of the thin and generally worthless seams of red hematite which are often found accompanying the limestones of the base of the Cincinnati or the top of the Trenton group, in East Tennessee. But, at the foot of the ridge, the Dyestone group again shows its two seams of ore. These cross the tramroad, just above the blacksmith's shop at the foot of the incline, and stand nearly vertical. The Devonian and Subcarboniferous shales and limestones, which follow, are overturned along their outcrop, and dip 52°, S. 30° E. The same dip was noticed in these beds on the bank of the Little Emory, at the mouth of D'Armond's Gap. This overthrow cannot, apparently, have extended far downward. The overthrow was evidently greatest at the Little Emory, where even Coal No. 5 (first below the Rockwood seam) fails to come to the surface the third time in the front fold of the strata. As we pass westward, the overthrow diminishes rapidly, and disappears before we reach Goddard's Gap. Beyond that point there is another front fold of the coal strata, though of less extent than on Little Emory, which may possibly be accompanied by another overthrow of the lower beds; but I have not examined them particularly in that neighborhood. Along most of the Ridge this double folding of the strata has not taken place, and the position is evident and simple. Near the Gap, and opposite the front fold, the beds near and including Coal No. 6 reach and even pass vertically near the top of the Ridge; but further west they come low down on its front face, and have a general dip of 58°, N. 30° W., which is continued in the overlying strata to the very crest of the Ridge, though beyond that point, from one to three of the overlying beds of sandstone are, in different places, bent from 10° to 20° beyond verticality. From this irregularity it would appear that no very extensive series of strata could have been on top of them at the time of their upheaval. Passing westward along the Ridge, we find the dip undulating; at one point falling to 30°, and again, as at Goddard's Gap, rising to 80°. Beyond the latter point it declines again to the average of about 60°; but the main coal seams are here beyond the crest of the Ridge, by reason of the great bend in its course."

At the mines an entry has been driven in for 210 feet through a stratum of dark ferny shales and heavy bedded and shaly sandstones, with a dip towards the north or northwest. At this distance the Rockwood seam (No. 6) is cut, and rooms turned to the right and left. The seam outcrops about 100 feet above the lower entry, and 636 above floor of the dump-house. The outcrop shows five feet, with a large thickness of dark clay shale below. Another entry was made twenty feet below the outcrop, and the two united by a slope through the coal. The coal is lowered over a double-track incline. This incline is about 1000 feet in length, and the cars are let down by a horizontal drum and iron or steel cable. From the foot of the incline to the rear, nearly two miles, there is a norrow-gauge tramway, over which one mule pulls six large cars. The coal at the dump-house is loaded in barges, and floated down the Big Emory to the Clinch and Tennessee rivers. The mines are worked now only to a limited extent. It is estimated that not over 10,000 bushels were taken from these mines for the year 1876.

The quality of the coal is said to be very superior. Prof. Wormley, of Columbus, Ohio, says, concerning this and coal taken from an upper thin seam, they are the best coals he has analyzed. His analysis is given below:

Specific Gravity	1.308
Water	1.50
Ash—light fawn color	7.70
Volatile matter	27.70
Fixed Carbon—coke compact	63.10
	100.00
Sulphur	0.53
" left in coke	0.45
Permanent gas per pound, in cubic feet	3.32

"The high percentage of fixed carbon here indicated," says Prof. Bradley, "together with the fact that the coal softens very little in the fire, shows that this would be a fine fuel for iron furnaces in the raw state. The unusually small percentage of sulphur is also exceedingly favorable for this purpose. This may perhaps be increased slightly in some portions of the seam; but the entire product of the mine is noticeably free from sulphur, at least in the form of pyrite. The sample sent for analysis was not selected for its purity, but was a full section of the seam, from roof to floor, cut from the top of the main entry near its extremity. It is therefore a fair sample of the coal as sent to market. Its lower surface has been exposed in the entry for nearly two years, but showed no sign of decomposition. I would have preferred a sample from a fresh cut, but none was at that time readily accessible. The exposure may have reduced the amount of both water and sulphur; but, from the wet condition of the roof of the entry, I judge that the change had been very slight. The very light color of the ash proves the amount of iron to be very small: it was not separately estimated. Piles of coal long exposed to the air show, on freshly-broken surfaces, the iridescence but not the color of the iron oxide which results from the decomposition of pyrite. As the superintendent of the Knoxville Gas Company certifies that this coal yields, in his retorts, 4.47 cubic feet of gas per pound, the yield of 3.32 cubic feet, shown in the analysis, may be taken as an indication that the sample sent had by exposure lost a part of its volatile matter. The Gas Company's test would show the unusually large yield of 10,032 cubic feet of gas per ton; while even the analysis shows 7,437 cubic feet, which, taken in connection with its unusual freedom from sulphur, makes this a very desirable coal for all gas companies who are not too far from the mines."

The coal taken from No. 10 shows well from the analysis given by Prof. Wormley?

Specific gravity	1.285
Water	1.50
Ash---light fawn color	2.60
Volatile matter	30.10
Fixed carbon---coke compact	65.80
	100.00
Sulphur	0.71
" left in coke	0.52
Permanent gas per pound in cubic feet	3.32

"As the portion of the seam whence this sample was taken has been hardly at all disturbed, the fine quality of the coal would seem to depend upon its original composition rather than upon the natural caking process, which has probably benefitted the lower seams. This seam, though occasionally thickening to two-and-a-half and three feet, as is said to have been frequently the case in the old workings in Tarkill Ridge, does not average over two feet in thickness, and occasionally thins out to one foot. Portions that are of average thickness, as is the case with the most of that on Laurel Branch, are too thin to be worked profitably by hand, but can probably be advantageously mined by machinery. The coal cakes in the fire more than that of No. 6, and would probably prove to be a superior blacksmithing coal. It is the hardest bituminous coal that I have ever seen, and would bear transportation with very little breakage. It is evidently a valuable gas coal. Though it cakes somewhat in the fire, it is probable that it could be used in the iron furnace, if mixed with coke. Coal taken from this seam at the old openings in Tarkill Ridge had a good reputation in Kingston, both for blacksmithing and for house use."

The seams of dyestone ore at this place have not been examined to any great extent. There are two all along the foot of Walden's Ridge. These vary in thickness from a few inches to four feet or more. Near Big Emory river two seams crop out and extend northward, showing themselves at the base of the synclinal. A few hundred dollars spent in prospecting would, doubtless, reveal as much iron ore at this point as at Rockwood, below, or Oakdale above. With iron ore, coal and limestone, all lying within half-a-mile of one another, no better site could be found for the erection of a furnace or a number of them. If such a locality were owned by the State, and a penitentiary established, it might solve the difficult question of what to do with our convicts. Employed in making iron, they would not come into competition with the mechanics or coal-miners, and the product of their labor might be considered raw material, to be worked up by the skill and ingenuity of the artisan. The erection and working of ten or fifteen furnaces would not produce a perceptible effect upon the price of iron. Such an establishment might be leased, and all the trouble arising from competition with the mechanics of the State avoided, as less than ten per cent. of skilled labor is required in the manufacture of pig iron.

OAKDALE FURNACE.

This furnace, though not lying immediately upon the line of the Cincinnati Southern Railroad, comes within the scope of territory proposed to be embraced in this report. It is situated ten miles north of Kingston, and about an equal distance from the railroad, and four miles east of the mouth of Little Emory River. The furnace was erected in 1873, and has a capacity of thirty tons in twenty-four hours. It was in blast only sixty-four days when the company suspended operations. The height of the stack is $63\frac{1}{4}$ feet, bell top, hot blast, bosh 16 feet, 4 tuyers, and a draught-stack 90 feet high. It has a battery of four boilers 50 feet long and 42 inches in diameter; a blowing engine with 2 steam cylinders $26\frac{1}{4}$ inches in diameter, and the blowing cylinder $68\frac{3}{4}$ inches diameter, with six feet stroke. The whole amount of iron made was 781 tons. Just before it ceased operation it was doing excellent work. A report for one week shows: iron made, 140 tons; consumption of coke per ton of iron, 102 5-10 bushels; ore per ton of iron roasted and raw mixed, 2 9-100; limestone one-half ton.

A tram-way has been built to the mouth of Little Emory, four miles long, by which the pig iron was carried out and loaded on barges for transportation down the river.

Quite a little village was built up around the furnace, consisting of two hundred and fifty houses, but in the absence of active operations very few are at present occupied.

The coal seams at this place have been attacked at three points—one of them in a spur of Walden's Ridge, and separated from it by a low gap; the other two in Walden's Ridge. The main entry, No. 1, is in the spur, and has been driven in through hard sandstone 280 feet, at which distance it cuts the almost vertical seam. At right angles from this entry a drift has been run 560 feet north-east, and another, 700 feet south-west, making a total of 1,260 feet on that level. At one place the coal disappeared for a short distance. The drift between was continued for a considerable distance without striking the coal, but it proved afterward that it was running parallel with the seam, a slight curve in the seam throwing the miners to one side. There are numerous horse-backs in the coal, and the thickness varies from a few inches to twenty feet. The coal is much crushed at places in this spur, as though the spur had been broken off by some terrible earth-throe, and the strata forced into one another, shivering and crushing the whole mass. The coal is by no means homogeneous; some of the specimens are very soft, and crumble in handling, while at other places the coal is a hard lump, and would bear shipping any distance. The dip of the seam is often reversed, but its general direction is toward the mountain. Two seams have been found in driving this entry.

As analyzed by E. H. Potter, the coal gives the followng result:

Fixed Carbon	56.150
Phosphoric acid	.640
Sulphur	1.207
Volatile matter	34.500
Ash	7.500

The entire product of this entry was 296,830 bushels.

Entry No. 2, is north-east of No. 1, nearer the summit. Very little coal was taken from this. No. 3 is two hundred yards from No. 2.

Walden's Ridge, proper, rises eight hundred and fifty feet above the valley in which the furnace is situated. The main mine to the west of Walden's Ridge is separated from it by a deep gulf, with very steep slopes. In this portion of the Cumberland Table-land the surface is very rugged, wild, and broken, with innumerable ridges and peaks standing boldly above the general level. Looking to the north-west from the top of Walden's Ridge, the landscape, covered with a dense forest, appears like a boisterous sea. Scarcely a single field can be seen for many miles. In this narrow, mountain-environed valley, between Walden's Ridge and the Cumberland Mountain, a few patches are cleared and cultivated by the hardy mountaineers. The wild mountain grasses are abundant.

The strata of Walden's Ridge, above Oakdale, are highly inclined—often perpendicular—and occasionally several degrees beyond verticality. Two coal seems have been opened in the south-eastern face of this ridge, which show a thickness of between three and four feet. A gorge intervenes between this and the spur from which most of the coal has been taken. There is no sign of coal in the north-eastern end of this spur.

There are three, if not four, seams of fossil ore to be found in the valley hills. The principal mining was done two miles south-west of the furnace. Here two seams are separated from each other by about forty feet of grayish shale. A shaft was sunk a considerable depth between the two seams, and drifts run out in opposite directions, striking the two seams. The seams at the outcrop were very thin, but at the depth of fifty feet they increased to eighteen inches. There were taken from this shaft, and another seam a mile further north, 4,480 tons. The two seams, between which the shaft was sunk, are probably the same, forming the outcrops of a decapitated fold. The two are said to unite five miles above the furnace.

The ore outcrops again nearer Walden's Ridge, with a general direction east of north. This is probably an outcroping of a synclinal fold on the east, as the Black shale and Siliceous group, with the mountain limestone are found in both ridges which lie eastward between this outcrop and the two already mentioned. This limestone was used as a flux in the furnace.

At Poplar Creek, four miles above Oakdale, there is a complete cut in Walden's Ridge, known as Winter's Gap. Three seams of coal have been opened here, one of which, in the main mountain, is seven feet thick. A good deal of coal was shipped, many years ago, from this point to Knoxville, Chattanooga, and Huntsville, Ala. It is thought to be equal, if not superior, to any coal in the State, being very hard, free-burning, and bearing shipment without loss. Mining is only done here now for local purposes. Coal is also mined, to a small extent, at Frost Bottom and the mountain fork of Poplar Creek.

Near this gap, in the valley behind Walden's Ridge, a salt well was bored one thousand feet deep many years since, and water obtained which yielded eight per cent of salt. The work on the well has recently been resumed, and it is confidently believed that large quantities of salt will soon be manufactured at this point.

The seam of dyestone ore maintains its persistency all the way from Oakdale to Winter's Gap, and up even to Cumberland Gap, keeping its intra-valley position throughout its course, making its length in the State quite one hundred and sixty miles, and capable of supplying ore for untold ages.

Retracing our steps now to Emory Gap, which is a cut through Walden's Ridge, we find the railroad taking this as its easiest and quickest ascent to the top of the Cumberland plateau. The strata in this remarkable ridge are here nearly perpendicular, but dipping in the usual direction.

It has been, and still is, a matter of doubt as to how far the inclined strata extend under the mountain. In digging out the foundation for the piers of the bridge in the bed of the river, a horizontal bed of dark shale was encountered in the direct line of Walden's Ridge, here cut away by ancient river action. The edge of this shale bed rests nearly perpendicularly against the upturned sandstone. The elevation of the road-bed here is 803 feet above tide water in Mobile bay, while the elevation of low water mark in Emory river is 728 feet. The bridge at this point will be 520 feet long, crossing the river at a considerable angle.

On each side of the railroad line, which follows the left bank of Emory river (the right going up), for three or four miles, are high bluffs, sometimes with steep escarpments, but more generally sloping down by the accumutions of talus to the water's edge. These are made of heavy and thin bedded sandstone, interstratified with micaceous sandy shales. After passing Walden's Ridge the strata take a very gentle dip to the north. The shales in places have a curled or rolled up appearance—at the outcrop folded around an axis, and resembling the bark of a dead tree. So perfect is the deception that in many places it is hard, without close inspection, to tell these curled masses from the trunks of imbedded trees.

The character of the country, after leaving Emory Gap, changes entirely. Here we have the carbonferous sandstone formation on both sides. No more cultivated farms are seen, and very rarely a house. The rough hills rise to various elevations above the railroad. Ascending these some plateau lands are found, extending in strips between elevated points, and often dissected by streams. The soil is sandstone, variable in its productive capacity, but essentially the same in composition. Its producing capacity is affected by location; sometimes, also, by the proportion of argillaceous matter in composition. This clayey matter adds to its fertility. Where there is an undue preponderance of sand it becomes very sterile. The soil from Emory Gap to the State line may be thus classified:

1. Thin sandy soil, resting upon sandstone, which comes near the suface. This is unfruitful, both from original poverty of constitution and from a want of depth. Very few trees attain any size upon this.

2. Sandy soil, light but deep. Upon this the wild grasses spring up, and retain their succulence until the heated months of July and August. The characteristic timber upon this is chestnut oak, interspersed with groves of yellow pine.

3. Sandy soil over a mulatto clay. This, by reason of the clayey foundation, which enables it to catch and preserve fertilizing material, is the best of all the upland soils of the mountain. It is very fertile upon the north hill sides, assuming in such places a black color very much like the black prarie lands of Texas, but more friable and not so waxey. Heavy timber of all kinds characterize this soil. Upon the level areas, where it prevails, extensive white oak forests occur; upon northern slopes, walnut, poplar, maple, hornbeam, hickory, buckeye, and black oak.

4. Alluvium along the water courses, black and friable, resembling the best lands on northern slopes, but of greater depth. Highly productive. Sugar maple, walnut, poplar, and shag-bark hickory delight in such places. These bottom lands are very narrow in the counties above Emory Gap.

5. Glade lands—the beds, probably, of ancient lakes—in which has accumulated vegetable material; soil black usually—sometimes ashen—always charged with humic acid to such a degree as to be unproductive, unless thoroughly drained and sweetened by aeration No timber is found in such places except such as will flourish in wet

soils. A few water oaks, the red flowering maple, and the sweet gum characterize such spots. When cleared a wild, coarse grass, known as bear grass, springs up. It properly belongs to the sedge (cyperacæ) family. This grass yields very largely, and has some nutritious properties. When properly improved, and seeded to herds grass, these glady spots will produce the most luxuriant crops for many years, often paying the total cost of their reclamation and improvement the first year. Thousands of these places are found all over the Cumberland Table-land, now lying worthless and unproductive, but which will ultimately be considered the most desirable spots for agricultural purposes in that division of the State.

Such are the general features of the section under consideration so far as the soils are concerned. As to the timber and cultivated crops, these will be noticed in detail as we proceed, together with the mineral deposits.

Passing along the line of the railroad northward the first coal occurs two miles and a half above the gap, the seam of which has been cut by the excavation. This coal is thirty inches thick. Lying above it is a heavy bed of bluish shales, and shaley sandstones below. The strata dip northwestwardly at an angle of fifteen degrees. This coal outcrops fifty feet below tunnel No. 26, which penetrates a massive layer of black sandy shale, that usually disintegrates rapidly when exposed to the weather. This tunnel is 1,600 feet long. Passing out of this tunnel northward a lower seam of coal, fifteen inches at the outcrop, appears on the right, dipping under tunnel No. 26. We enter the mouth of tunnel No. 25, at the distance of about two hundred and fifty yards. Right at the mouth of this tunnel is a local fault, where a great protruding mass of sandstone has been uplifted, throwing the coal seam above the top of the tunnel. Beyond the tunnel, which has been driven through this uplifted sandstone, the coal seam comes down again to the level of the road-bed. The coal here lies between the sandstones, shales appearing above, separated from the coal by twenty feet of sandstone. The dip toward the north-west, is reversed a hundred yards above the tunnel.

Three miles above tunnel No. 25, is another seam, probably lower geologically than either of the others. This seam rests upon a shaley sandstone, with twenty-five feet of buff colored slates above, then thin and heavy bedded sandstone, the same, probably, under which occurs the coal two and a half miles above the tunnel. The coal at this latter place lies in a low synclinal, the seam being about three feet thick. The character of the coal is good. Applications have been made to the officers of the road to drift into the seam at right angles to the road-bed, but as this would interfere with the stability of the slopes of the cut, it was refused. A shaft could be sunk on the slope above, and the coal taken out by a drum, and dumped into the cars on the track below.

Outcroppings of coal seams are reported on the right and left of the road. Generally, the thickest outcrops lie back from the road a few miles, and occur at or near the foot of the hills resting upon the general plateau.

North of tunnel No. 25, the strata show as much disturbance as the minor ridges in the valley of East Tennessee. This continues up to tunnel No. 24, a short distance above. This tunnel is cut through a remarkable bed of black shale, or slate, whose cleavage is perpendicular to the plane of stratification. The face of this strata is almost as smooth as ice, presenting the appearance of a solid wall of masonry on the side of the approach to the tunnel. Near the center of this tunnel the sandstone comes down from the top four or five feet, and forms the sides and top of the tunnel. There is a fault, also, immediately over the tunnel, the sandstone having dropped down in a perpendicular fracture. This tunnel is 2,030 feet long. The next tunnel, No. 23, a mile or two above, is cut through sandstone, and is 800 feet long. At tunnel No. 22, there is a good seam of coal thirty inches thick on the sandstone above the tunnel. This tunnel passes through dark colored shale. Two miles above a horizontal seam of coal, eighteen inches thick, appears on the left of the road-bed between strata of shales, with heavy bedded gray sandstone below. This sandstone is excellent for building purposes, and is used by the engineer in charge in constructing culverts and protecting walls. Here an extensive quarry has been opened, the strata being perfectly horizontal.

WARTBURG AND VICINITY.

Wartburg, the county seat of Morgan county, lies three miles to the east of this point, and is a place deserving of some mention, on account of its location, and the experiments which have been made in the vicinity in the growing of fruits. The town is situated 1,500 feet above the sea, on a considerable plateau which extends southward for ten or twelve miles to the breaks near Emory Gap. This plateau is traversed by occasional ravines and deep gorges, hemmed in by precipitous sandstone bluffs. On the northeast Ward's Mountain looms up in majestic proportions about 1,200 feet above the town, and 2,700 feet above the sea. It is a long, rounded-top ridge, whose general course is north-east and south-west. Its slopes are densely clothed with forests of excellent timber, consisting of chestnut, chestnut-oak, pine, and black gum. On the north-western slope many walnut trees are found. On a tract of 5,000 acres, lying on its top and sides, 340 large walnut trees have been counted. The following were counted by Drury Smith at another point: Forty-seven walnut trees, four feet and over; seventy-eight, three feet and over; one hundred and thirty-two, two feet and over, and one hundred and forty-eight of one foot and over. Two trees were measured five and six feet respectively. North-east of Wartburg, on the head waters of the Emory river, and east of the line of railroad, on the line between Morgan and Scott counties, there are large bodies of walnut timber in the coves and on the northern slopes. The soil is very fertile, but so much broken as to preclude cultivation. It would make excellent grazing lands, for which purpose it will no doubt be ultimately used. The coves running up into this mountain are very fertile. Even upon its crest farms have been opened, and the soil is said to yield generously, producing even more than the soil of the mountain-valleys below. Chalybeate springs break out from its top.

The reader should constantly bear in mind that these peaks, or ridges, lie upon the general top of the Cumberland plateau—mountains piled upon a mountain.

Lone Mountain rises to the south-east of Wartburg, four miles distant. Pilot Mountain, eight miles to the northwest, is said to be the highest point in the vicinity. East is Chimney Top, nearly as high as Pilot Mountain. Southwest, across Emory River, is Crab Orchard Mountain. This range of mountains, extending south-west into Cumberland county, is cut into three unequal parts by two gaps. The highest peaks of this mountain is 1,000 feet above the general level of the table-land. East of Wartburg there is a considerable area of mountain-valley lands, on Mud Creek and Flat Fork, tributaries to Emory river, hemmed in by Ward's Mountain on the west and Brushy Mountain on the east. These valleys are of moderate fertility, and may be considered highly productive for mountain lands. The soil is frequently water-soaked and white. A spur runs down into this valley from Ward's Mountain on the north-west. Flat Fork runs at the western foot of Brushy Mountain, which is the northern prolongation of Lone

Mountain. Brushy Mountain is noted for the excellence of its timber. The walnut timber was so abundant on its western slope that it was used for making fence rails.

Wartburg was settled by Germans many years since. These people planted out large orchards and vineyards. The apple trees have done well, and bear vigorously, and the finest specimens of apples may be found here of any place in the State. Several years ago the apples from this place took the premium at the fair at Nashville.

The failure of the grape crop has had a depressing effect upon those engaged in horticultural pursuits. Vineyards were planted with the expectation of manufacturing wine, but there has been only two or three good seasons for the grape at this place in twenty years. It is quite probable that the grape would do well upon the slopes of the mountain, while it would prove a failure in the intervenient valleys. Peaches fail two years out of three. Pears do better. The smaller fruits, such as cherries, gooseberries, and strawberries, are said to be more certain in their yield than any of the fruits except the apple.

Among the field crops rye gives the most generous returns. The usual yield is from fifteen to eighteen bushels per acre. The growing of Irish potatoes and onions, with proper care and attention, can be made profitable. Irish potatoes are a staple crop. From one hundred to one hundred and fifty bushels are raised per acre. Sweet potatoes are not extensively cultivated, and will not compare in excellence with the Irish potatoes. Indian corn, on the best soils, will make from fifteen to twenty bushels per acre; oats about the same. Very little wheat is grown —not enough for home consumption. Rye bread, however, supplies its place to a considerable extent. Hay is made from timothy and herdsgrass. The yield is small. Sometimes the wild mountain sedge is cut and cured for feeding cattle in winter.

The yellow mulatto, clayey and gravelly land is considered the most productive. It is found in mountain sags and coves, and on northern slopes.

With the means of transportation at hand, the farmers of Morgan county could turn many things to profit which are now neglected.

The trade of Wartburg is confined to a very few articles that will bear transportation over the rough roads of the country. Feathers, beeswax, ginseng, wool, and fruits, constitute the principle exports. There are four dry good stores, three churches, two schools, and two cabinet maker shops in the place.

Some excellent coal is found in the vicinity of the place. Jones' Bank, lying four miles east of the town, has a seam thirty-four inches thick. It yields a very fine block coal, the best I have met with anywhere. The seam is horizontal, and crops out in one of the mountain valleys. The coal from this place supplies the demand at Wartburg. Coal has been opened at several other places, and the seams are much more promising here than those near the railroad. And this is generally true in Morgan and Scott counties.

From Triplett's Gap to New River.

Triplett's Gap lies on the railroad, four miles north-west of Wartburg. The country between the places is level, with a sandy soil, and a good growth of timber, pine and black oak predominating.

At Triplett's Gap a commissary department was kept up, and the vegetables exhibited, all grown in the county and on the table-land, were as fine as can be seen in any market. The cabbage showed large, compact heads, not excelled by any brought from the North. The onions and Irish potatoes, also, were unsurpassed by those grown in any country. The apples were plump, round, and large—many of them weighing fifteen ounces.

The tunnel at Triplett's Gap is cut through black shale, filled with nodules of the carbonate of iron, so abundant as to form probably an eighth of the material removed. Just above Triplett's Gap a considerable pine forest sets in on both sides of the road, and continues for two or three miles. This gives place to a white oak forest, which is almost unbroken to the State line. The forests of white oak are of peculiar value. The timber is of medium size, rives easily, but is very heavy and close grained. Glades are of frequent occurrence on each side of the road. These glades grow wild grasses luxuriantly, and thousands of sheep can be kept on these mountain grasses at a nominal cost. This part of the table-land, extending from Wartburg north, greatly resembles Wales in aspect and in the character of its soil. The scenery from the elevated peaks has great picturesque beauty, and will, no doubt, in time, attract many visitors. It will also be the home of the herdsman; and butter, cheese, wool, beef, mutton, and fruit will form no inconsiderable articles of export. In Wales the Hereferd cattle are prefered, and this breed, or the Devon, would no doubt be found very profitable in this rough mountain region.

The coal exposures on the line of the road from Triplett's Gap to the State line are usually thin and unimportant. A seam is exposed at Tunnel No. 17, a foot or more thick. The surface above this tunnel continues for some miles, broken, with but few level areas. The timber, mainly white oak, increases in size and value—that on White Oak creek is very fine. This is a tributary of Board Camp, which empties into New River of the Cumberland. The shales above White Oak creek are remarkable for their beautiful violet colors and micaceous specks, much resembling the metamorphic slates of the Ocoee group. This violet shale disintegrates less rapidly than the black. Clay iron-stones are abundant in every cut through the shales.

Black Wolf creek is in Scott county, and comes from the west side of the railroad. It empties in Clear Creek, an affluent of New River. Upon Black Wolf the timber is very heavy. Large white oaks and poplars send their long columns more than 100 feet into the air, equalling in size the princely white oaks and poplars of Obion county, in West Tennessee. The soil grows better, and is not so broken. The land is well suited for the production of tobacco, and efforts will be made by some farmers to plant largely of this crop.

On Black Wolf creek some good seams of coal have been opened. One of these is over three feet thick. Three miles north of Black Wolf creek the country becomes very rugged, and New River is approached by a tunnel 2,580 feet long, cut through gray shale and sandstone. New River is the principal tributary of Big South Fork of the Cumberland, it taking the latter name after its confluence with Clear Fork. The bridge over New River, with viaducts, will be 1,300 feet long, and 125 feet high. There will be three spans, two of 90 feet each, and one of 200 feet. The approaches will be made by iron viaducts.

Upon the plateau lands, to the north-west, beech trees are quite abundant—a very unusual occurrence upon the table-land. So far as one may judge of the character of the crops, the soil might be considered of a better quality than the plateau lands on other parts of the mountain. Very little sand is seen A yellow clay forms the subsoil, and the native growth denotes considerable fertility.

New River supplies some valuable water privileges. There are seven or eight mills situated upon it within Scott county. Its tributaries—Buffalo, Brimstone, Clear Creek, Clear Fork, Phillips Creek—all furnish more or less available sites for mills.

Huntsville and Vicinity.

Huntsville, the county seat of Scott county, is situated near New River, three miles east of the line of railroad. It has a population of about 80. Its business is very small. Two dry goods stores, two groceries, one blacksmith shop, and two taverns, constitute nearly all the business houses. There is one church, and, sometimes, a school.

The range of Jellico Mountains lies on the north-east, and Round Mountain on the South. These mountains have a soil of exuberant fertility, as the character of the timber will indicate. Walnut, poplar, buckeye, ash and locust, are common. The locust grows near the top of these billowy mountains, walnut in the coves, and poplar on the northern slopes. The best lands in the county are found upon Jellico Creek, which, rising in the mountains of the same name, flows northward into the Cumberland. The bottoms on Brimstone are quite wide, and of very great fertility. The native growth of these bottoms is mainly beech. Buffalo Creek has also some cultivable bottoms, as also Pine Creek. The lowlands, lying upon New River, are generally narrow, but fertile.

The northern slopes of Jellico Mountains yield sometimes as much as forty to fifty bushels of corn, fifteen of wheat, and twenty of rye, per acre; producing nearly or quite as well as the bottoms upon the streams; but the fertility does not last, as it is impossible to prevent washing on the sharp slopes. Next to the bottoms and north hill-sides, in point of fertility, the swales succeed. The soil of the swales is white and clammy, but produces herds-grass and millet excellently well. A. J. C. Robbins, a railroad contractor near Huntsville, has made some experiments with deep culture. On mountain lands, by the application of a small quantity of manure and deep plowing, he made forty bushels of corn and two hundred bushels of potatoes per acre.

Bull Creek and Smoky enter New River from the north. On these streams walnut trees are abundant, many of them measuring three feet in circumference. The county east of Huntsville will be spoken of under the head of Knoxville and Ohio Railroad.

Farming lands are cheap in Scott county, and a drug in the market. Good average farms, improved, are worth from five to ten dollars per acre; unimproved mountain lands, suitable for colonization, from fifty cents to two dollars per acre. Defects in titles should be guarded against. Unfortunately for this mountain region, there are often four or five grants from the State of Tennessee to the same tract.

Around Huntsville several valuable coal banks have been opened for local uses. One of these is a little north of the town, and the coal crops out in a swale on the west side of a considerable elevation. The seam is three feet thick, and the coal is cubical, hard, and very pure. Another bank has been opened on Flat Creek, between Huntsville and the railroad. Flat Creek is a wet-weather stream, with a high sandstone bluff on the south side. It has its drainage in New River, with a general south-east course. The coal crops out under the sandstone bluff, with a thick bed of shale beneath. It is three feet thick generally, but the seam is variable. It is also a block coal, but crushed at places. Up the same ravine, three-quarters of a mile, Potter's bank has been opened. It is the same seam.

From Huntsville to State Line.

The scope of country embraced between Huntsville and Chitwood, directly north and west of the former place, is not so rugged. No deep cuts are found on the railroad going north until Flat Gap is reached, where there is an excavation fifty feet deep. There is a low depression also between the head waters of Pine Creek and Bear Creek, both tributaries of South Fork. The character of the soil and timber is much the same as that found below Huntsville. Chitwood is the name of a locality three miles south of the State line lying immediately on the railroad. North and west of this place the surface is deeply cut by streams, with flat crested ridges between. Towards the north-west it assumes more of a plateau character, with some soils of more than average fertility. This plateau land extends south-westerly to New River, beyond which are many spurs pointing down to the river. East of Chitwood are the Jellico Mountains, drained by Jellico Creek, Elk Fork and Cove Creek—the latter breaking off in an opposite direction into the waters of the Tennessee. Paunch Creek flows near Chitwood, and empties into South Fork. There are wide bottoms on this stream, but the soil is cold and clammy. Nearly all these smaller streams go dry in summer, only a few pools remaining in their beds, which, however, supply good stock water, For domestic purposes wells are resorted to, and water is always found at a moderate depth, pure and sparkling, and generally with a slight chalybeate taste.

White and yellow pine are abundant on Pine Creek. Chinquapins, chestnuts, hickory nuts, several varieties of wild grapes, persimmons and blackberries grow in profusion.

From Huntsville to Jamestown.

Returning now to a point on the railroad opposite Huntsville, and passing to the west in the direction of Jamestown, the county seat of Fentress county, we pass over numerous streams, the principal ones being South White Oak, North White Oak and Clear Fork. The latter forms a junction with New River, after which it takes the name of South Fork of the Cumberland. The country becomes very level towards Jamestown, which is thirty-two miles east of Huntsville. The soil is sandy and thin, but, with careful culture, will make from twenty to twenty-five bushels of corn. Large forest of yellow pine occur, and tar and turpentine were extensively manufactured before the war. Many fine forests have been ruined by scalping the trees, in order that the crude turpentine might exude. Fires are of frequent occurrence in the woods. These attack the combustable exudations upon the trees, and burn out great hollow places in the trunks, destroying their value as timber trees. The highland pasturage, however, by reason of the open woods, is excellent, and cattle and sheep may be grown at a very small cost. It is almost impossible for a farmer to regulate the quantity of his stock. He has summer pasturage for unlimited herds, but it is difficult to grow provender enough to carry them through the winter. Farmers living in the rich valleys herd their cattle upon the plateau of the mountain from April to October, when they are carried to the valleys and wintered. The rearing of live stock is the only profitable branch of agriculture on the thin mountain lands. The character of the stock is beginning to be improved. Some Cotswold and Southdown sheep have been brought in, also a few Berkshire hogs.

Coal is found in many places around Jamestown. Southwest of this place, two miles in Rockcastle Cove, there is a seam four feet thick, of good quality. East of Jamestown, on Crooked Creek, outcrops of coal are numerous. On Buffalo Cove Creek there is a seam exposed three to four feet thick. Also at the head of Buffalo Cove the same seam appears. Near the head of East Fork some very thick seams are said to exist. On White Oak, at Step's, an outcrop of fine block coal has been worked. This coal is very hard and beautiful. Ten miles west of Jamestown there is an oil spring. Another similar spring is found three miles higher up. There is no question but petroleum could be found in any quantity by boring; and when the railroad is finished this branch of mining will receive the attention its importance demands. Some iron ore exists in the county, and also a coarse, reddish marble. The iron is found about nine miles south of Jamestown.

Jamestown, the county seat, is on the "divide" between Obey's River, on the west, and Clear Fork, on the southeast. It has three stores, two groceries, one cabinet shop, two taverns, and two schools.

From Jamestown to Crossville.

From Jamestown to Crossville, the county seat of Cumberland county, thirty-six miles, the country is generally very level. As elsewhere, the streams all flow in rocky "gulfs," or gorges, varying in width and depth according to the size of the stream. Sometimes these gorges are from one to two miles wide, showing the enormous erosion which has taken place since the deposition of the sandstone and shaly strata that make up the mountain mass. The conglomerate rock comes very near the surface. The region under consideration is generally a flat area, thickly set in timber, with but a small amount of cleared land. The principal timber for eight miles south of Jamestown is pine, chestnut, and spotted oak. At this distance the ravines and slopes of the head waters of Clear Fork begin. These ravines are separated from one another by long, winding strips of plateau lands. The slopes are clothed with white oak, hickory, chestnut oak, poplar, and dogwood. Several places were seen on the plateau, between Jamestown and the head waters of Clear Fork, where the chestnut timber, originally very large, has died out entirely. This is attributed to the ravages of the bore worm. At many places the dead trunks were standing over hundreds of acres, as though they been belted by the axe of the woodman.

Passing the ravines going south we ascend the great divide between the Tennessee and the Cumberland rivers.

The old stage road between Knoxville and Nashville passed, and the line of railroad between the two places laid out, on the crest of this water-shed. On this divide there is a very great quantity of white and yellow pine, the white pine being confined to the small creek basins. White oak forests are also met with, sometimes continuing for miles. The almost total absence of other kinds of timber in these forests is a little remarkable. North of the Nashville and Knoxville road, and west of the railroad, this region, as far north as the Huntsville and Jamestown road, and as far west as the Jamestown and Crossville road, is much cut up by ravines made by the head waters of Clear Fork and Emory river. The timber in this rough region is very large. Walnut, white pine, white oak, yellow poplar, cherry, and buckeye are found in greater or less quantities. Pine Orchard is a locality in the fifth and sixth civil districts of Morgan county, ten or fifteen miles west of the railroad, and on the head waters of Little Clear Creek. It is so called from the large quantities of valuable pine timber covering, in the aggregate, over one hundred square miles. Scarcely any other trees are seen. Many of the pines have trunks seventy or eighty feet long and three feet in diameter.

The soil in Fentress and Cumberland counties is more sandy than in Scott and Morgan. The clayey and productive soils are met with on the north hill-sides, and here the patches and farms are opened. The plateau lands, though delightful in their appearance, are shunned. The consequence is that but few farms are opened on the high ways. On the road from Jamestown to Crossville, for the distance of eighteen miles, there are only four houses to be seen. And yet these plateau lands are well adapted to the growth of fruit. Wherever an orchard has been planted, though the farm may have been abandoned, yet the fruit trees look vigorous and bear abundantly. Apple trees are often seen in old fields almost breaking down with the tempting fruit. Oats and vegetables also make a certain crop. With the mountaineers, however, corn is the great desideratum. Their daily food consists of mast-fed bacon and corn bread. Wherever, therefore, they can make supplies of corn they go, even though it be inaccessible for wheeled vehicles. Some of the plateau land, where a heavy turf has been formed, produces corn the second and third years after being opened—the corn plant being fed by the decaying turf. After the third year no reliance can be placed on it for that purpose, the fertilizing matter filtering down through the porous sand. The northern exposures of the ravines often produce twenty-five bushels of corn per acre; rye, ten bushels. Potatoes are not more productive here than on the plateau lands. They are usually grown upon manured lots near the dwellings, and the yield is sometimes incredible.

Clear Creek of Obed's river, makes a wide deep cut in the Table-land. Beyond this, going south, are open woods, small timber, but standing thickly upon the ground; black oak mainly. The principal crops grown on the plateau are buckwheat, sorghum, and oats. The grazing privileges are unexcelled. No calacanthus, ivy, or other poisonous shrub is seen. Chestnut timber is very scarce, the older trees having died out and the smaller ones killed by the annual fires. There are many hickory glades. Crossing Obed's river, a tributary of the Emory, four miles north of Crossville, we come upon a thinly wooded region, abounding in wild grasses and excellent water. This would be an admirable place for herding cattle during the summer. This thinly wooded region covers here several hundred square miles, and extends south of Crossville eight or nine miles. Scrubby blackjacks and small postoaks constitute the principal trees.

It may be mentioned that every stream in this region, which furrows its way to the lower strata, exposes seams of coal. There is coal on Meadow Creek, Laurel Creek, Potts Creek, Drawing Creek, No Business, Clear Creek, and numerous others. Brown's bank and Andrews' bank have been opened on Laurel Creek, a tributary to Caney Fork. The coal for the blacksmiths shops in Crossville is obtained from this place. It is a hard block coal, and looks well. Eleven miles south of Crossville occurs a curious depression on the Table-land, known as

GRASSY COVE.

This depression is about four miles long, and contains about 5,000 acres. It lies on a line with Sequatchee Valley, and the coal measures have been eroded and washed away down to the limestone of the subcarboniferous. The cove is depressed three hundred feet below the average elevation of the table-land. The soil is limestone and fertile. There are about forty families living in this cove. This remarkable indentation is in the fold of Crab Orchard Mountain, which lies between Emory river and the head of Sequatchee Valley. As before mentioned, it is cut into three unequal parts by Crab Orchard Gap and Grassy Cove. At Crab Orchard Gap, north-east of Grassy Cove, the severance is complete, leaving room for an extensive farm between the abutting ends, while at Grassy Cove there is a wearing away of the strata so as to make a deep broad depression. The Crab Orchard Mountain, resuming its course at the south-western extremity of the cove, continues in a direct line to the head of Sequatchee Valley. The strata of the table-land are horizontal, or approximately so, at its western end, but as one approaches toward the east they lose their horizontality in part, and are found crowded into folds. The first important fold is Crab Orchard Mountain. It is, indeed, the same fold that produced Sequatchee Valley, only it was not broken open on the back. In the highest part of this mountain the fold rises seven or eight hundred feet above the general level of the table-land, the strata of the mountain forming an arch. By this means limestone in places has been brought on a a level with the table-land. The water from Grassy Cove collects in Grassy Cove creek, which finds its way under the mountain, by a subterraneous passage to the head of Sequatchee Valley, a distance of four or five miles. This stream has a sufficient volume of water to drive a mill. This cove constitutes the best area of farming lands to be found in Cumberland county. Stock raising is carried on to a considerable extent. Mr. Richard Marston, of England, is engaged here in breeding Shropshire-down sheep, and Mr. Stratton in raising Devon cattle. The latter gentleman has been experimenting with grade Angora goats, and finds them quite profitable. They live throughout the year upon the shrubs that grow on the mountain slopes. He estimates the cost of the flesh not to exceed one cent per pound. He raised seventy-five kids with less trouble and expense than an equal number of chickens.

One of the finest presentations of coal in the State is to be seen four miles south-east of Grassy Cove, on the head waters of White's creek, and about eight miles west of the line of road. This coal bank is in Cumberland county, and is known as McCall's bank. It is eleven feet thick, with a horizontal bed of shale above. The coal shows some disturbance. Occasionally masses of shale are found imbedded in the seam. The coal rests upon a bed of fire-clay, the thickness of which could not be determined without considerable expense. The coal much resembles the Rockwood in appearance and general structure, though it is some harder, and will bear shipping with less loss. The seom outcrops 192 feet below the road on the top of Walden's Ridge.

Swaggerty's Cove is another indentation in the Crab

Orchard fold between Grassy Cove and the head of Sequatchee Valley. On the slopes of the mountain surrounding this cove is as large timber as can be found in the State. It would be very valuable if not so difficult of access.

Passing over another ridge, we enter Sequatchee Valley This remarkable valley is about seventy miles long and four miles wide, and is rich in agricultural and mineral wealth. The Knox group forms the centre of the valley, with the Trenton rocks in strips on east side. The Dyestone group and mountain limestone hug the mountain escarpments. On the east side of the valley there is almost an unbroken seam of dyestone ore, varying from one to six feet thick. Great beds of calc spar also occur on the same side. On the opposite or western side of the valley, coal is found up every notch in the mountain. Through the centre of the valley, which will average about four miles in width, the Sequatchee river flows, supplying sufficient water power for all economical purposes. Here, within a limited area, are found three of the greatest levers of human civilization—fertile lands, coal and iron. Here can be united in the most profitable relations, and on the most extensive scale, the producer and consumer. A great system of manufacturing industry should spring up in this valley, compelling the raw material to serve the purposes of commerce, and contribute to the wealth and greatness of the State. At present, under the stimulating effects of an English company, a railroad is being built by the Nashville and Chattanooga Railroad Company, up the valley, from Jasper, at its foot, to the Victoria mines, a distance of eight miles. This road will convey coal to the works at South Pittsburg, where quite an extensive town is laid out, and foundations for furnaces laid. Everything is done in the very best style.

The productiveness of the soil of this valley is well known.

Here all the cereals and grasses find a congenial home; and the large number of hogs and cattle annually driven out to Chattanooga and other points, justify the assertion that no better farming lands are to be found in the State. It is estimated that 3,000 beef cattle and 12,000 hogs are annually fattened and driven out this valley.

With a railroad running up to the head of this valley, and passing over Walden's Ridge to connect with the Cincinnati Southern, the lower half of our coal field will be ribboned with railway lines, from which arms may be thrown out, and the entire southern half of the coal field made available to our people and profitable to the State. At present these coal fields add but little to the revenue of the State, being assessed at from ten to fifty cents per acre. With proper exertion on the part of our people, both in their corporate and individual capacity, these lands may yet pay off the State debt by increased valuation. In Indiana, such lands as these roads will open, are rated at from one hundred to three hundred dollars per acre, and capital from various parts of the country have been attracted thither for profitable investment. In Pennsylvania, lands in the same coal field, with the identical seams, sell for as much as one thousand dollars per acre. In the State of Tennessee, although the coal lies contiguous to iron ore of first-rate quality, ten dollars per acre for coal lands would be considered an exorbitant price. With the opening of these railroads, and a proper presentation of the resources that lie on these routes, it is to be expected that these lands will command such a price as their inherent value justifies.

SOUTH OF TENNESSEE RIVER.

Walden's Ridge, south of the Tennessee River, takes the name of Racoon Mountain. Here the mountain is much cut up by deep ravines, and its continuity is almost destroyed. Nevertheless, some good coal seams, both on the upper and lower coal measures, are found on this side of the river. The principal mines opened are the Ætna and Vulcan, both lying in Marion county, on the Nashville and Chattanooga Railroad; the first about thirteen miles west of Chattanooga, and the latter sixteen. Battle Creek mines are on the Jasper branch of the same road, and the production of coal amounts to 19,500 bushels per month.

ÆTNA MINES.

Raccoon Mountain, in which these mines are opened, rises about 800 feet above the bed of the Nashville and Chattanooga Railroad. Upon its top is a plateau with a superimposed ridge. which contains two seams of coal. The section as given on pages 98 and 99 will show the various seams at this place, with their thickness, and the thickness of other strata.

It will be seen that there are five seams below the lower conglomerate, two between the upper and lower conglomerate, and three in the upper coal measures. The first seam from the bottom has never been worked. The second, known as the Mill Creek seam, is opened on the right of Mill Creek, about one mile from the railroad. The thickness of the coal varies from two to three feet. The coal is laminate and lustreless. The entry has been driven in about 700 feet, fifty-four degrees west of north. Below the coal occurs a black shale. The coal and shale often run into and intertwist with each other in wavy lines, sometimes one and then the other disappearing. Below the shale are ripple-marked flagstones and sandy shales, with nodules of clay iron-stones. In some places in this entry the upper surface is horizontal, and six or eight inches of good block coal lies against the roof. Below this the coal is more shelly and soft, with a contorted lamination. In a cross entry, running north and south, which has been driven to the right, is seen a great wall of shale that crosses the entry at an angle of about twenty degrees. The roof in this entry has an arched appearance in places, and at others is wavy and irregular, with convexities. The bottom is generally smooth.

Cross entries are made on each side of the main entry alternately, 150 feet apart. A block of coal, 27 feet wide is left on each side of the main entry to support the roof. Rooms are turned every nine yards from the cross entries.

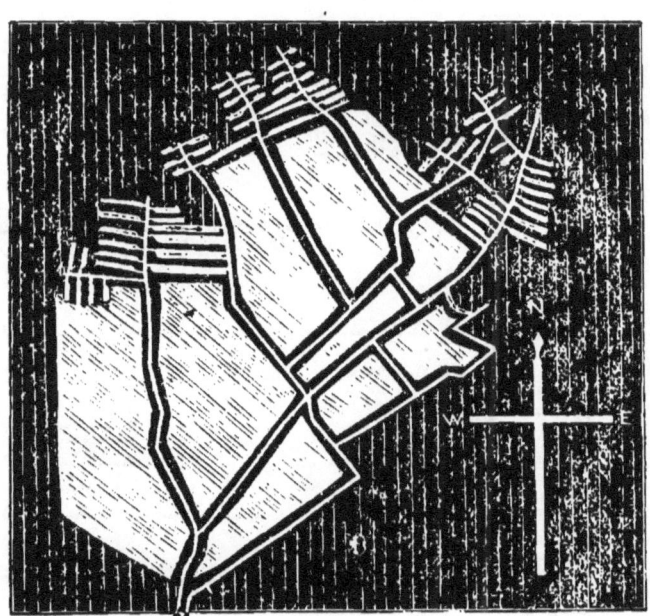

Horizontal Plan of Ætna Mines—Kelly Seam.

The Kelly seam, the seventh from the bottom and the third from the top, has been opened about two feet above the railroad. It has been more extensively worked than all the others combined. About twenty acres of coal have been taken out. This is, doubtless, the equivalent of the Sewanee; at least it occurs about the same horizon. The

Total in Ft. & In.		Section.	Materials.	Ft.	In.
			Surface...	5	6
			Sandstone..	75	0
116	0		Shaly Sandstone..	32	0
			COAL—Oak Hill..	4	0
167	6		Shale and Thin Coal..................................	46	0
			COAL—Slate Vein......................................	566	6
			Shale..	44	9
214	11		COAL—Kelly Coal......................................	2	8
			Fire Clay..	1	6
			UPPER CONGLOMERATE...................... (Simply a Sandstone.)	82	6
298	1		COAL..	0	3
			Yellow Sandy Shale	45	4
			Gray Shale...	47	8
391	11		COAL..	0	10
			Gray Sandy Shale	45	0
			LOWER CONGLOMERATE .... (Cliff Rocks)	95	0
534	11		COAL—Main Ætna..................................	2 to 5	0
			Fire Clay..	2	2
			Shale, resembling Hickory Bark..............	20	0
557	11		COAL..	0	10
			Gray Shale..		

Total.		Section.	Continued.	Ft.	In.
			Gray Shale..	95	6
653	11		COAL	0	6
			Black Shale.....................................	20	0
676	3		COAL—Mill Creek vein	2	9
			Fire Clay...	3	0
			Shale with nodules of Carbonate of Iron	40	0
			Gray Shale......................................	34	6
756	3		COAL—Lowest Bed	2	1
			Fire Clay...	2	3
868	3		Shales and Shaly Sandstone..............	109	9
			Limestone.......................................		

seam is continuous, and varies in thickness from twenty to forty-eight inches. At the distance of six hundred yards in the mines a basin occurs in the coal seam, which covers probably six acres. Towards this basin the coal inclines, and increases in thickness. The water interferes so much, that the coal from this basin will have to be worked from a perpendicular shaft. The mine is drained by a pump; capacity forty gallons per minute.

The coal, when taken from the Kelly mine has no superior in the State. It shows a fibrous structure across the plane of lamination. The laminæ are often separated by seams of mineral charcoal. The coal is very pure, burning with a brilliant glow, and making an intense heat, leaving as a residum about two-and-a-half per cent. of fawn-colored ash. The following analysis of this coal was made by Julius G. Pohle, of New York:

Volatile and bituminous matter...............................	21.39
Carbon in coke...	74.20
Sulphur...	70
Ash---fawn color...	2.70
Moisture	1.30
	99.99

Specific gravity..................... 1.281

Dr. Pohle says:

"The coal is well adapted to gas-making so far as the quality of the bituminous matter is concerned, but the quantity is not so great as the coal usually used for that purpose. which latter usually yields from forty to fifty per cent. of volatile matter."

About 130 men are employed in these mines, fifty of whom are miners. When employed by the day, the miners receive two dollars and fifty cents. Usually the coal is mined at a price depending upon the thickness of the seam, varying, however, from sixty-five cents to one dollar and twenty cents per ton. Common laborers are paid per day one dollar. The driving of entries is let to the highest bidder, but the coal taken out is paid for separately.

The coal is brought down from the mountain to the Nashville and Chattanooga Railroad by three inclines:

First—One thousand feet of track, nearly level, from the mouth of the Kelly mine to the head of a steep incline.

Second—A gravity plane, 3,500 feet long, running from the termination of the first to a stationary engine on Mill Creek.

Third—A track extending from Mill Creek to the screens on the railroad, 3,700 feet long. A steel cable is used in letting down and drawing up the cars.

The facilities for loading cars at the railroad are very great. There are numerous shoots with screens, having an aggregate capacity of 500 tons per day. For furnishing locomotives an ingenious contrivance has been perfected by which trains are stopped but a few seconds, the coal being weighed in lots of fifty bushels, and shipped into the tenders from a shaft by lever action.

There are eighty-three coke ovens, having a capacity of 1,500 bushels per day, though the actual amount of coke made rarely exceed half that amount. One hundred bushels of coal will make one hundred and twenty bushels of coke. The coke is very hard, and will bear up any weight desired. It is mainly used in foundries, and brings from fifteen to seventeen cents per bushel. Bartow Furnace, in Georgia, is supplied with coke from this place. The coal taken from these mines brings a higher price than any other mined in the State. Lump coal, loaded on the cars, sells for 12 cents per bushel; fine coal, for blacksmith purposes, $12\frac{1}{2}$ cents; run of the mines, 11 cents. The coke and coal from these mines are shipped to New Orleans, St. Louis, Louisville, and even as far as Texas. The New Orleans, St. Louis and Chicago Railroad takes ten car loads per month for their shops. The coal taken from the Mill Creek seam makes a coke much inferior to that taken from the Kelly seam above. A considerable amount of coal from the Kelly seam is used for gas at Chattanooga, Huntsville, Atlanta, and Augusta.

A little village has been built up near the railroad; and upon the plateau above, at the mouth of the Kelly mine, some forty houses have been erected for miners. They are rented from one to three dollars per month.

The following table will show the shipments for the year ending August 31:

SHIPMENTS OF COAL FROM ÆTNA MINES FROM SEPT. 1, 1875, TO AUG. 31, 1876, INCLUSIVE.

1875.	Bush.
September	59,346
October	53,668
November	51,642
December	53,935
1876.	
January	25,800
February	34,691
March	55,346
April	33,921
May	36,714
June	42,820
July	39,571
August	56,133
	$543,587

Vulcan Mines.

These mines have been opened in the northern extension of Sand Mountain, seventeen miles west of Chattanooga, immediately on the line of the Nashville and Chattanooga Railroad. They are owned and operated by the Bartow Iron Company, of Georgia. A tramway 1,400 feet long brings the coal down to the railroad. Thirty coke ovens have been constructed, but only six are in repair.

The lower seam worked at this place corresponds with the Mill Creek seam at the Ætna mines. This seam here varies in thickness from a few inches to five and a half feet. The thick coal usually occurs after a "squeeze." The strata here are very irregular, occurring in rolls and horsebacks. The coal lies between strata of black shale very hard. The shale is highly bituminous, and much of it will burn as well as peat. Below the underlying black shale is a hard sandy shale. This coal is irregular in its structure. At the top and bottom it is very hard, but in the center of the seam it frequently exhibits a crushed appearance, the laminæ showing wrinkles. Where squeezes occur a thin seam is generally left, which serves as a guide. These squeezes rarely extend more than ten yards when going at right angles to it. The coal is often mixed, in consequence of these squeezes, with the overlying shale. Sometimes this shale is interstratified with the coal, especially where the coal is thick. The further the entry is driven in the mountain the thicker the coal. The average of eight measurements of the seam is $3\frac{1}{8}$ feet. The top of this mine is not very good. This seam is worked altogether by convicts, and the estimated cost of mining is between fifty and sixty cents per ton of twenty-eight bushels.

The Ætna seam above the fourth from bottom, in the Ætna mines, has been worked for many years. It was formerly worked at the Ætna mines, but is now abandoned at that place. This has a wide spread under the lower conglomerate, or cliff rock. It is very irregular in thickness, varying from sixteen inches to four feet; occasionally sinking to a few inches. The coal has seams of mineral charcoal between its laminæ. It is a good lump coal, and is used in gas works and for blacksmith purposes. The seam will average probably twenty-two inches in thickness. For digging, eighty cents, ninety cents, and one dollar, is paid per ton. The first price for digging where the seam is two feet and over; the second for twenty-two inches and over, and the third where the seam falls below twenty-two inches. Only free labor is employed in working this coal. The quantity now taken out does not exceed one hundred and fifty bushels per day. The coke made from this coal is very pure, and sells for fifteen cents per bushel. That made from the lower seam is rough, full of shaly material, and very inferior.

About sixty-four men are employed at the Vulcan mines, forty-one of whom are convicts.

The quantity of coal and coke mined and shipped from these mines for the year ending Aug. 31, 1876, was 305,280 bushels. Of this less than one-tenth was coke. The coal from the upper, or Ætna seam, sells for 11½ to 12½ cents per bushel; that from the lower seam from 8 to 9 cents. The average daily production to the man employed, is forty-eight bushels.

The Kelly seam, and the two above, as shown in the Ætna section, are wanting at this place.

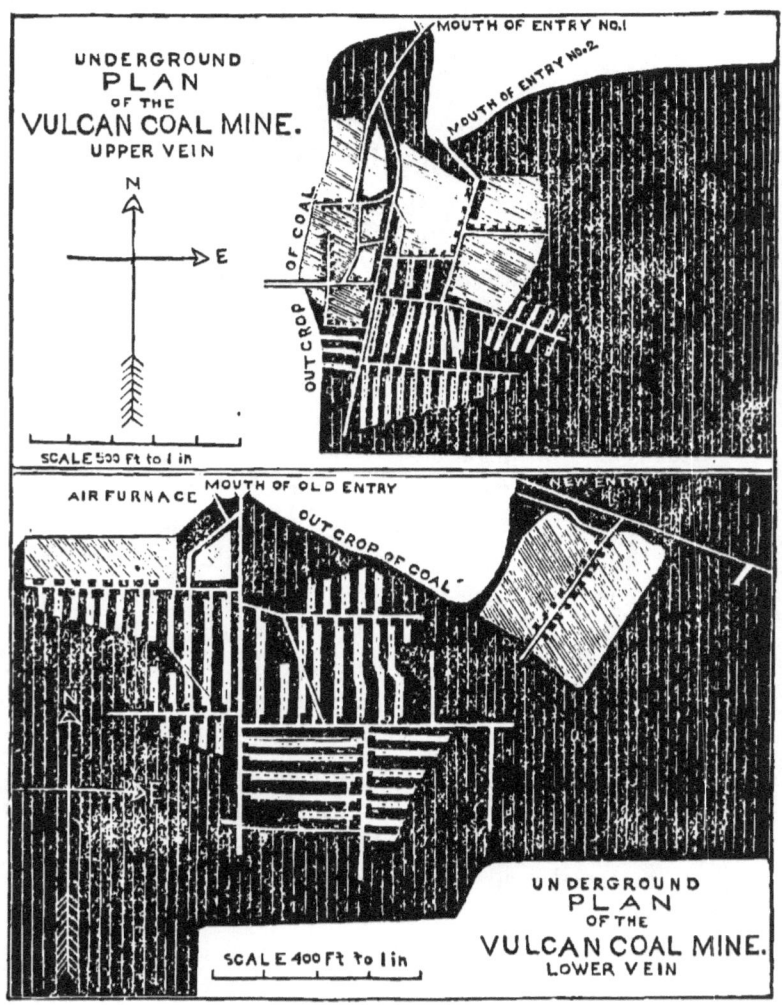

KNOXVILLE AND OHIO RAILROAD SECTION.

We now propose to direct attention to a portion of the Tennessee coal and iron fields that are in rapid process of development, which a connecting link with the Cincinnati Southern Railroad, by way of Morrowville and Poteet Gap, will immensely hasten.

The Knoxville and Ohio Railroad takes the general direction of north-west from Knoxville to Careyville, in Campbell county, and has been completed to that point, a distance of thirty-eight miles. The road has been graded for eight miles further, to a point near Morrowville (Buckeye Tavern). A preliminary survey was made from this point to the Cincinnati Southern Railroad, by Major Ernest Ruhl, and submitted to Col. C. M. McGhee, President of the Knoxville and Ohio Railroad. This report contains so much information in regard to the topography of the country between the two roads, and is of such general interest, that I give its more important parts, as well as the estimates given for the construction of the connecting link by several routes:

The main obstacle in the way of the connection, says Major Ruhl, in his report, is the problem of overcoming the divide between the waters of Tennessee and Cumberland rivers. In my opinion there is only one feasible point where this can be accomplished, and this is Poteet's Gap. The balance is comparatively light work for a road through such a mountainous country.

The point of divergence from the Knoxville and Ohio Railroad, formerly located through Elk Gap, would be at the confluence of the two main prongs of Cove Creek; one heading at Elk Gap and the other at Poteet's Gap, a place known by the name of Buck-eye Tavern (Morowville).

The country north-west from Buck-eye Tavern consists of several chains of high mountains---Buffalo, Jellico, and Beach mountains---causing a direct line from Buck-eye Tavern to the Cincinnati Southern Railway to be infeasible, as it would require one continuous tunnel with an occasional gap for ventilation. It may, therefore, be assumed as a fact that any connecting line between the Knoxville and Ohio road and the Cincinnati Southern has to take the route through Poteet's Gap.

The main difficulty about Poteet's Gap is the fact that there is no valley, not even a ravine, heading at the west side of it; that the line has to cross the valley of Straight Fork about half a mile west from the summit, and that the difference in elevation between the gap and the valley is three hundred and forty feet.

A line was run from Poteet's Gap about one mile up Straight Fork; thence crossing the valley, down again on the west side, for the purpose of increasing distance, thus to be enabled to overcome part of difference in elevation by grade. The idea was abandoned because the work required for construction proved to be heavy; but principally on account of the narrowness of the valley, necessitating a semicircular curve of less radius than is permissible on a safe railroad.

There are two ways of overcoming the difficulty in the line through Poteet's Gap and the immediate crossing of the adjoining valley of Straight Fork. One is by a tunnel of about four thousand feet in length and an embankment fifty feet high for four hundred feet in length, thence from fifty feet in height decreasing gradually to nothing in two hundred and fifty feet distance on each side of the short high fill. The other method is by a tunnel of one thousand eight hundred feet in length and iron trestle work one hundred and fifty feet high for about four hundred and fifty feet in length, thence from one hundred and fifty feet in height decreasing to forty feet in height in about five hundred feet distance on each side of the highest part of the structure, thus aggregating one thousand four hundred and fifty feet of iron trestle.

The relative cost of the two proposed plans is about:

4,000 feet tunnel in soft material, 13½ cubic yards per linear feet, at $2¼ per cubic yard		$135,000
1,333,333 feet B. M. timber at $35 per 1,000		46,666
Packing		5,334
Total for tunnel 4,000 feet long		$187,000
Adjacent embankment 70,000 cubic yards barrow, at 30 cents per cubic yard		21,000
Total		$208,000
Iron trestle 1,450 feet long, ...	$100,000	
1,200 cubic yards dimension mass	18,000	
Iron trestle	$118,000	
Tunnel 1,800 feet long	84,000	
Total		$202,000

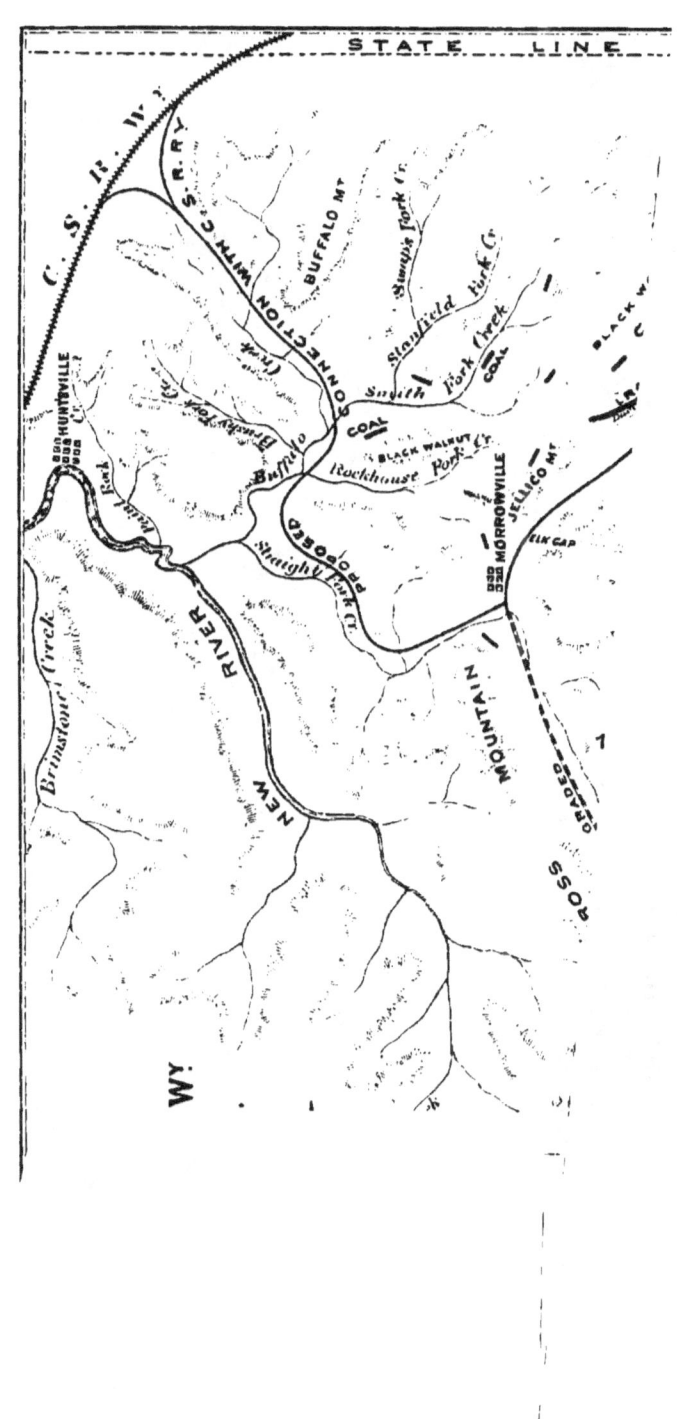

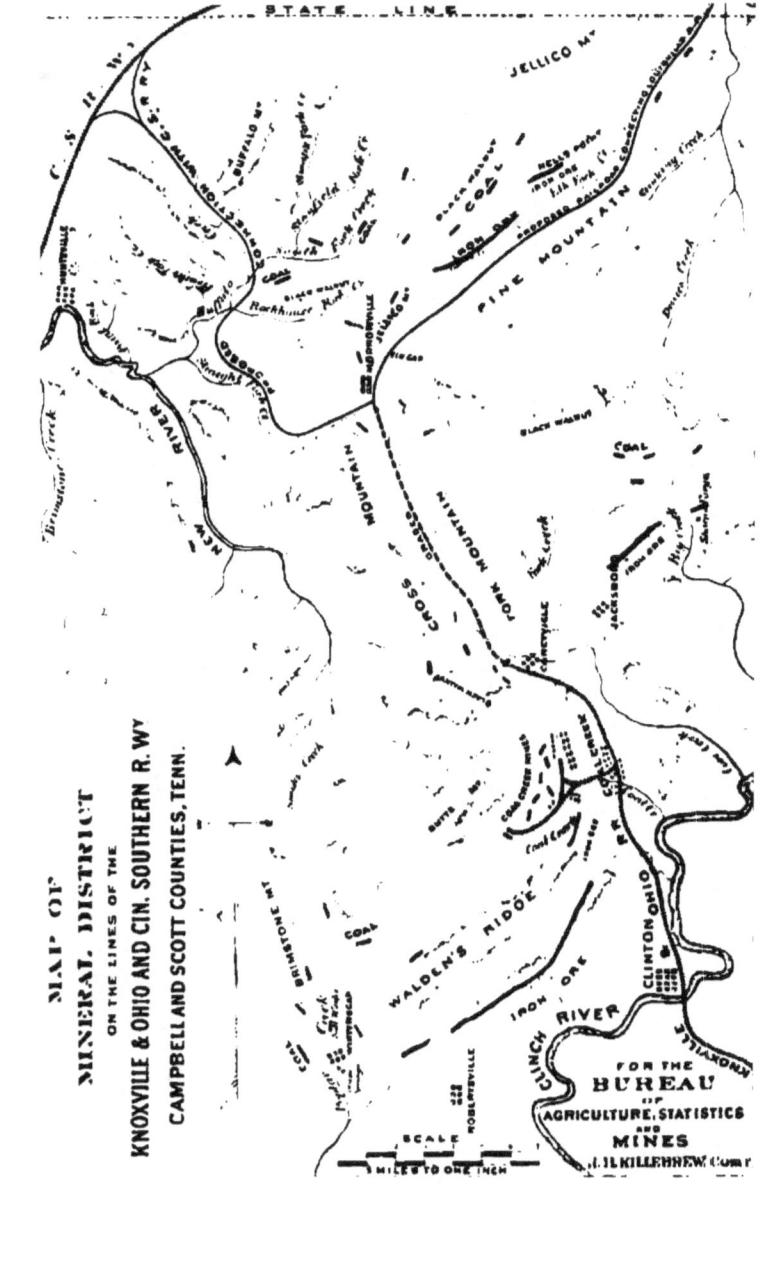

The difference in elevation of grade between the two lines being one hundred and two feet, the lower line will decrease the work west of crossing of Straight Fork over the higher one to a larger amount than the difference in cost between the long tunnel and the high trestle with short tunnel will come to.

But there is no necessity of executing immediately either of the above proposed plans, as a temporary track might be constructed on a grade sixty-six feet to the mile at a reasonable cost, thus getting the road in running order without being delayed by any tunnel, as the balance of the road can be built and operated in less than twelve months from the time of breaking ground. It would likewise defer the expenditure of a large sum until the road is able to sustain itself and pay for its improvements. For temporary track there would be required east of Poteet's Gap, to overcome two hundred feet in elevation, a distance of three miles; on the west side, to overcome three hundred feet in elevation, a distance of four and a half miles; in all seven and a half miles. The probable cost of it would be:

For grading, about $3,000 per mile..$28,800
Cross-ties and track-laying, $1,500 per mile............................ 11,150

$33,750.

This amount of $33,750 covers all the positive loss that would occur after the permanent road is built, as the iron can be taken up from the temporary track and used again.

After reaching once the water of Straight Fork the road will have to follow it to Buffalo creek, down that creek to New River, thence down New River to the mouth of Paint Rock creek.

As above stated, there is only one feasible route as far as Paint Rock creek. Between the crossing of Buffalo creek and Paint Rock a tunnel six hundred feet in length will be necessary to avoid following a horseshoe bend in the river. The balance of the work is of such a character as will cost, on a portion of the Cincinnati Southern Railway, through a country of similar topography, about $20,000 per mile. The tunnel of six hundred feet in length will cost about $28,000.

The distance from Buck-eye Tavern to Paint Rock is twelve miles.

In order to make the connection at the New River crossing of the Cincinnati Southern Railway, the line keeps the slope of the river bluff from the mouth of Paint Rock, with the exception of two bends in the river, which need not be followed, the ground laying in a more direct line being favorable to locate the road on. The whole distance from Paint Rock to the Engineer's office at New River is seven and a half miles. Two miles of it may be estimated at about $25,000 per mile, and the balance, of five and a half miles, at about $20,000 per mile.

The line passing through Huntsville, and forming a connection near Newport, will have to cross Paint Rock creek on a bridge ninety-five feet high, with approaches of iron trestle-work, costing in all about $22,000. Between Paint Rock and Huntsville a tunnel will be required of eight hundred and sixty feet in length, costing about $40,000. The distance from Paint Rock to a point on Cincinnati Southern Railway, near Newport, is six miles, of which two miles will cost about $25,000 per mile, and the balance, of four miles, $20,000 per mile, exclusive of the $62,000 for tunnel and crossing of Paint Rock.

The line to form connection near Dick Smith's, like the one joining the Cincinnati Southern Railway near New River, will require a bridge across Paint Rock of only such elevation as to be above high water. Of the different branches of Paint Rock examined, I prefer Keeding's Fork for the line. The distance from the mouth of Paint Rock creek to the intersection with Cincinnati Southern Railway, near Dick Smith's, will be ten miles. Through Smith's Gap in the divide between Paint Rock and Pine creek, a tunnel of about eight hundred feet in length will be necessary, costing $37,000. The first three miles from the mouth of Paint Rock up, may be estimated at $25,000 per mile; the upper seven miles at $20,000 per mile.

Below will be found an approximate estimate, and a summary of the different routes, as given by Major Ruhl:

ESTIMATE OF COST FROM CAREYVILLE TO PAINT ROCK.

Repairing road-bed from Careyville to Buck-eye	$20,000
Iron, ties, and track-laying, at $9,000 per mile	72,000
Total from Careyville to Buck-eye	$92,000
Work on Poteet's Gap	208,000
Tunnel between Buffalo and Paint Rock creek	28,000
Grading from Buck-eye to Paint Rock, 12 miles, at $20,000 per mile	240,000
12 miles track from Buck-eye to Paint Rock, at $9,000	108,000
Total from Careyville to Paint Rock	$676,000

ESTIMATE OF COST FROM CAREYVILLE TO NEW RIVER JUNCTION.

From Careyville to Paint Rock		$676,000
From Paint Rock to Engineer's office, grading	$160,000	
Seven and half miles track	67,500	
Total from Paint Rock to Engineer' office		227,500
Grand total for New River connection		$903,500
Estimate of permanent work at Poteet's	$208,000	
" temporary " "	90,000	
Deduct difference between permanent and temporary		118,000
New River Junction actual necessary outlay		$785,500

ESTIMATE OF COST FROM CAREYVILLE TO NEWPORT JUNCTION.

From Careyville to Paint Rock		$676,000
High trestle and tunnel near Paint Rock	$62,000	
Grading 2 miles, at $25,000; 4 miles at $20,000	130,000	
Track for six miles	54,000	
Total from Paint Rock to Newport Junction		$246,000
Grand total for Newport Connection		$922,000
Deduct difference between temporary and permanent work at Poteet's		118,000
Newport Junction actual necessary outlay		$804,000

ESTIMATE OF COST FROM CAREYVILLE TO SMITH'S JUNCTION.

From Careyville to Paint Rock		$676,000
Tunnel at Smith's Gap	$37,000	
Grading 3 miles, at $25,000; 7 miles at $20,000	215,000	
Track for ten miles	90,000	
Total from Paint Rock to Smith's Junction		$342,000
Grand total for Smith's Connection		$1,018,000
Deduct difference between permanent and temporary work at Poteet's		118,000
Smith's Junction actual necessary outlay		$9000,00

SUMMARY OF THE DIFFERENT ROUTES.

Point of connection on Cincinnati Southern Railway distant from line.	Miles of new road to be built.	Entire cost of permanent work, including repair of grades and track from Careyville to Cincinnati Southern Railway.	Entire cost of making connection from Careyville to point on Cincinnati Southern Railway with temporary track through Potcet's Gap.	Distance from Knoxville to Cincinnati.
At Emory Gap, 256 miles from Cincinnati.	40 miles.			296 miles.
Near crossing of New River, 216 miles from Cincinnati.	19½ miles.	$903,500	$785,500	282 miles.
Near Newports, 213½ miles from Cincinnati.	18 miles.	$922,000	$804,000	278 miles.
Near Dick Smith's 206 miles from Cincinnati.	23 miles.	$1,018,000	$900,000	274½ miles.

This connecting link would lie wholly within the coal measures, and would open a country hitherto unknown, but destined in the future to add immensely to the wealth of the State.

COAL CREEK COAL MINES.

After leaving Knoxville, the Knoxville and Ohio Railroad cuts a number of ridges of the Knoxville formation at right angles, passing these, generally through low gaps or by deep cuts, tapping the coal field at Coal Creek, thirty miles above Knoxville, crossing the Clinch River at Clinton. At Coal Creek Station Walden's Ridge is cut by Coal

Creek, which comes out from the mountain at right angles. Through this cut a branch railroad, half a mile long, has been built up to the mines, which have been opened on the main mountain, back of the gap. In the little back valley two streams, one from the north and the other from the south, unite to form Coal Creek. They meet, and the combined waters flow out at right angles to the tributary streams. The general section, as given by Prof. Bradley, shows twenty-one seams of coal at this place, ten of which are of workable thickness. The total aggregate thickness is thirty feet. The entire thickness of the coal measures is about 3,000 feet. The seam worked is the fifth from the bottom, and is about 140 feet from the bed of the creek. It varies from four to seven feet in thickness, and supplies a cubical coal that presents a very handsome appearance when carried to market. Not more than one-tenth is lost in mining and handling.

Five companies are actively engaged in mining at this place, viz.:

Anderson County Coal Company.
Knoxville Iron Company.
Black Diamond Company.
Franklin Company.
Empire Company.

The mine of Anderson County Coal Company is situated a half mile south of the Black Diamond mine. The main entry is driven in about 260 yards—direction south 70 west. Twelve yards from the mouth an entry was turned to the left, running south 25 east; then turns in the same direction as the main entry. At the distance of fifty yards another entry is turned south 70 east, running in that direction for about 100 yards, when it takes the same parallel course with the other two. The rooms are turned on the left of each entry, and twelve yards apart. The following section of the coal was taken on the inside:

Roof, Hard Black Shale, Thin.	Ft.	In.
Coal	0	4
Shale	0	1
Coal	0	2
Shale	0	1
Coal	2	0
Shale	0	1
Coal	1	6
Total thickness of Coal	4	0

The fire clay at the bottom is hard and sandy. The coal dips slightly south 75 west, but the mine drains itself, the coal being worked in every instance upward. This company employs fifty persons generally; thirty-five of them are miners. Royalty to the owner, from whom the property is leased, one cent per bushel. Cost of mining, $2\frac{1}{2}$ cents for mixed and 3 cents for lump coal.

President, E. C. Camp, general manager, Knoxville; C. O. Ward, agent, Coal Creek.

The mine of the Knoxvile Iron Company has an entry for the distance of 286 yards, bearing south 75 west for that distance. Afterwards it turns to the left for 250 yards to an entry that runs parallel to the first. The main entries are driven seven and a-half feet wide, and five and a-half to six and a-half feet high. Cross entries are turned at 108 yards apart, of the same dimensions as the main entry. The rooms are all turned to the right, and are worked through to each cross entry. The rooms are fourteen yards wide, leaving a pillar of six yards between each room and the entries. The coal here has also several shale partings, as is shown by the section below Beginning at the top:

Roof, Hard, Tough Black Shale.	Ft.	In.
Coal	0	5
Shale	0	3
Coal	0	$2\frac{1}{2}$
Fire Clay	0	$1\frac{1}{2}$
Coal	1	6
Shale	0	2
Coal	2	3
Soft Shale	0	5
Bottom Coal	0	10
Total thickness of Coal	5	$2\frac{1}{2}$

The method adopted in mining here deserves mention. No blasting powder is employed. The three-inch shale seam next to the upper coal is picked out, and the five inches of outlying coal prized down. This is carried in for five or six feet. Then the second parting is taken out, and the coal below prized up. This process is continued until all is removed. By this means the coal is not shivered to such an extent as when blasting powder is used, and the blocks can be taken out in almost any size. There is a very small proportion of slack, not exceeding one-tenth of the coal taken out, even after going through all the handling necessary to get it upon the cars ready for shipment to market.

The roof, composed of hard black shale, rarely breaks down. The bottom is hard fire clay, interstratified with thin sandstones. The coal dips a little west of north; therefore, all cross entries are turned to the left. The coal is brought to the mouth of the mine on wooden tracks of three-feet gauge. Some of the entries are laid with T rails, 11 lbs. to the yard. This company employs forty miners and about thirty other persons, and ships about 90,000 bushels per month. Royalty one cent per bushel. Miners are paid $2\frac{1}{2}$ cents per bushel for mixed coal and 3 cents for lump coal.

Major W. R. Tuttle, Knoxville, manager; M. Llewellyn, agent at Coal Creek.

The Black Diamond mine is situated about one mile south and west from the last mentioned. The main entry, driven under the spur of Butt Mountain, bears south 53 west, and runs in this direction for 70 yards; then turns south 37 east for the distance of 400 yards. There are four cross entries turned to the right, 45 yards apart, and nearly all the rooms are turned to the left. The section taken in this mine shows:

	Ft.	In.
Coal	0	4½
Shale	0	3
Coal	1	9
Shale	0	1
Coal	1	1
Shale	0	1
Coal	0	8½
Shale	0	3½
Coal	0	10
Total thickness of Coal	4	9

The top is a hard, tough shale; bottom, fire clay, very hard. The same system of mining is carried on here as at the mine of the Knoxville Iron Company. This company employs sixty-five persons, forty of whom are miners. Miners are paid the same rates as paid by the other companies mentioned. Fifteen car loads, or 3,750 bushels, are taken out daily from this mine, or an average of 83 bushels for each miner employed. The monthly shipment will amount to about 64,000 bushels.

The Franklin mine was not examined, but is understood that the top is bad, and the coal has two shale partings, one eight inches thick, and another six. The lower parting has coal below one foot thick. The seam, including the shale partings, is four feet thick. This company employs sixty persons, forty of whom are miners. The average daily production of coal is five car loads, or 1,250 bushels, which shows a small average for the number of men employed. During the month of October the shipments amounted to 23,750 bushels.

The Empire mine is situated on the east side of Butt Mountain (a local name given to a rounded projection of the main mountain) 400 yards north of the mine of the Knoxville Iron and Coal Company. The main entry, at the distance of 150 yards, has a cross entry to the left. This entry has three others turned to the left and three to the right. The rooms are on the right and left, and are worked upon the same system as the other mines in the locality. Sixty-five persons find employment in this mine, forty of whom are miners. Eight car loads are the daily production. The shale partings occur in this as in the Franklin mine. The amount of coal shipped in October was 190 cars, or 47,500 bushels.

These three mines last mentioned are under one management:—W. S. Geers, superintendent, Coal Creek; James Frazer, agent, Knoxville.

The wages of miners have been given. For drivers and outside hands, from one to two dollars per day is paid; boys, 75 cents.

I am indebted to Edward P. Moses, of Knoxville, for the subjoined statement (commencing on next page) pertaining to the coal trade of the Knoxville and Ohio railroad.

116   *Resources of Tennessee Along the*

It will be noticed that the shipments from Coal Creek and Careyville have been consolidated. A very large proportion was shipped from Coal Creek, the shipments from Careyville having been, in 1873, 14,676 tons; in 1874, 6,371 tons; in 1875, 3,774 tons: and in 1876 (first ten months), **only 494 tons**; so that we may say all the coal now transported is mined at Coal Creek.

COAL TONNAGE from COAL CREEK and CAREYVILLE in the YEARS 1873, 1874 and 1875.

DESTINATION.	1873.	1874.	1875.	Increase in 1875. Over 1873	Increase in 1875. Over 1874	Decrease in 1875. Under 1873	Decrease in 1875. Under 1874	Total Increase in 1875. Over 1873	Total Increase in 1875. Over 1874
Points South of Dalton...	36,880	15,416	22,090	....	6,674	14,790	....	....	....
Points North of Bristol ...	1,216	677	1,183	....	506	33	....	....	....
Points West Chattanooga,	1,647	332	78	....	....	1,569	254	....	....
Chattanooga and Points between Chattanooga and Knoxville	3,449	2,025	3,202	....	1,177	247	....	....	....
Bristol and Points between Bristol & Knoxville	2,039	1,993	5,222	3,183	3,229	....	....	....	....
Knoxville	15,951	22,744	34,368	18,417	11,624	....	....	....	22,956
Total...	61,182	43,187	66,143	21,600	23,210	16,639	254	4,961	

Coal Tonnage from Coal Creek and Careyville for year ending Oct. 31, 1876............ 73,431 tons.
  Do.   do.   do.   do, ... 59,500 tons.
           Increase in year ending October 31, 1876......... 13,931 tons.

COAL TONNAGE from COAL CREEK and CAREYVILLE in FIRST TEN MONTHS of 1874, 1875 and 1876.

MONTHS.	1874.	1875.	1876.	INCREASE IN 1876.		DECREASE IN 1876.		TOTAL INCREASE IN 1876.	
				Over 1874.	Over 1875.	Under 1874.	Under 1874.	Over 1874.	Over 1875.
January	3,166	4,857	4,623	1,457	....	....	234	....	....
February	3,119	3,822	5,072	1,953	1,250	....	....	....	....
March	2,128	3,988	5,603	3,475	1,615	....	....	....	....
April	598	2,671	4,355	3,757	1,684	....	....	....	....
May	2,018	1,738	3,434	1,416	1,696	....	....	....	....
June	1,418	2,973	4,401	2,983	1,428	....	....	....	....
July	2,002	5,349	3,997	1,995	....	....	1,352	....	....
August	3,944	6,625	7,565	3,621	940	....	....	....	....
September	6,315	8,949	8,468	2,153	....	....	481	....	....
October	8,394	9,695	10,441	2,047	746	....	....	....	....
TOTAL	33,102	50,667	57,959	24,857	9,359	....	2,067	24,857	7,292

COAL TONNAGE from COAL CREEK and CAREYVILLE in FIRST TEN MONTHS of 1874, 1875 and 1876.

DESTINATION.	1874.	1875.	1876.	INCREASE IN 1876.		DECREASE IN 1876.		TOTAL INCREASE IN 1876.	
				Over 1874.	Over 1875.	Under 1874.	Under 1875.	Over 1874.	Over 1875.
Points South of Dalton............	13,487	19,175	13,616	129	....	....	5,558	....	....
Points North of Bristol	587	1,094	567	....	....	20	527	....	....
Points West of Chattanooga......	302	58	70	....	12	232	....	....	....
Chattanooga and Points between Chattanooga and Knoxville..	1,683	2,283	2,009	326	....	....	274	....	....
Bristol and Points between Bristol and Knoxville...............	1,588	3,360	10,306	8,718	6,946	....	....	....	....
Knoxville........................	15,455	24,698	31,391	15,936	6,693	....	....	....	....
TOTAL......	33,102	50,667	57,959	25,109	13,651	252	6,359	24,857	72,92

CAREYVILLE MINES.

Careyville is situated at the terminus of the Knoxville and Ohio Railroad, near the foot of Powell's Valley, and thirty-eight miles from Knoxville. Cross Mountain rises on the west 3,123 feet above the village, and continues in a northerly direction to Morrowville. Fork Mountain, separated by Cove Creek from Cross Mountain, lies on the north of the town and continues its course nearly parallel with Cross Mountain.

The strata of Cross Mountain are nearly horizontal, having a slight inclination toward the south-west. Crossing the valley the strata show great disturbance, folded along two axes, one corresponding with Cross Mountain and the ether with Powell's Valley. The latter axis, further up the valley, is found two or three miles from the foot of the mountain. Near Careyville it approaches so closely as to give a sharp dip to the strata. The Cross Mountain axis, a few miles to the south-east, comes so near the mountain as to cause Walden's Ridge to consist of sharply inclined strata of both sides of the anticlinal. This anticlinal passes to the very bottom of Cove Creek, where the strata are found outcropping on edge, but in the mountain opposite Cove Creek, the strata are left in an undisturbed position. Where the two axis join near Careyville the strata are much confused.

The rocks of Cross Mountain pertain to the coal measures, two thirds of Fork Mountain, and a part of Cove Creek valley. Inclosed in the strata of Cross Mountain are, according to Dr. Safford, nine seams of coal, six of which he thinks are workable. I am of opinion, after a careful examination, that the thickness of some of those seames, as given by Dr. Safford, is local; for higher up on Cove Creek the thickness is considerably reduced. This opinion is likewise concurred in by Prof. Lesley, of Pennsylvania, who made a survey of this region, and a portion of whose report will be given hereafter.

Three workable seams, however, exist beyond all question, and should the one opened upon the top of Cross Mountain (at the outcrop ten inches) prove workable, there will be four. The outcrop of the seams are deeply covered on the mountain slopes by masses of sandstone. Prof. Bradley, to whom I acknowledge my obligations for many of the facts embraced in this report, thinks it probable that the lower two seams belong to the lower coal measures, and those above to the upper.

The lowest seam here is thought to be the equivalent of the seam worked at Coal Creek (coal E of Bradley's section), in which opinion, however, Prof. Lesley does not concur. This seam at Careyville lies nearly on a level with the railroad, and is about four feet thick. Three mines have been worked at this place, all opened in this seam.

The Careyville mine within a few hundred yards of the depot, was worked for several years, but is now abandoned. Two are now in active operation—Kennedy and East Tennessee—but they are not worked to any great extent, mainly for local use, as will be seen by reference to the table of shipments from this place. The Kennedy mine lies three or four hundred yards to the south of the Careyville mine. The seam shows the effect of the anticlinal to the east, the coal dipping at the outcrop to the north-west, but becomes horizontal within the distance of thirty yards, and afterward lies in a series of long waves. The seam where now worked has a parting of fire clay eighteen inches thick, with thirty inches of coal below and eighteen inches above. Sandy bluish shales lie below and a black shale above. There is a rise in the strata between the Careyville mine and this by which the coal at the Kennedy mine is elevated about ten feet above that of the Careyville mine. The main gangway of this mine is three hundred and fifty yards long, and runs nearly south. A cross entry to the shaft, made for ventilation, shows that the coal rises about three inches to the yard. From this cross entry at the distance of eighty yards from its begining point, another cross entry, running south, has been made, which follows the direction of a sharp ridge and under it, the drift being upon the fold of an anticlinal, the coal dipping downwards to the east and west. The shaft which has been mentioned goes through twenty-seven feet of loose standstone and gravel, forty feet of gray shale, eighteen inches of coal, and seventeen feet of fire clay to the coal now worked.

The coal in the sharp ridge spoken of, dips south four degrees east for about one hundreds yards, when a succession of short waves, or wrinkles (rolls of the miners) occur. These continue for about fifty yards, when a sudden drop, or fault, of twenty-five feet occurs, after which the coal rises gradually two inches to the yard.

These faults and rolls form a part of the East Tennessee mine, which has been opened about half a mile south of Careyville. A great many difficulties have been met with at this mine. The entry has been made at the end of a cove, or cul-de-sac, which sweeps around in a semicircle. The fault occurs at the distance of fifty or sixty yards from the mouth of the mine, and runs in a semicircle concentric with the range of elevations outside. In many places within the mine small seams of coal are found rolled up with the sandy shale. The main seam has a parting of fine dirty coal near the center. This is picked out, and the coal above prized down. The lower layer is then taken up. No powder is used in mining. The coal is thinly laminated and glossy; softens greatly in the fire.

Another opening has been made near the saw mill, and is known as Elliott's mine. The lower half of the seam only is in place, according to Prof. Bradley, who made a survey of this region, the upper half, though once deposited, having been washed away.

Quoting Prof. Bradley: "The entry has been carried in to the distance of three hundred and seventy feet, without again encountering any sign of thick coal. It is possible, however, that this erosion was only local, and that by following the thick coal from the point where it was encountered near the mouth of the mine, the full thickness would be encountered at nearly every point. The coal thus far brought from this mine, has been inclined to split up into thin laminæ, but this is apparently only the effect of some slight degree of weathering, the entry having skirted the lower spur instead of having penetrated it. The coal of this seam is usually quite free from pyrite (the sulphur of the miners. Other openings are now being made to test this seam.

"*Second Seam.*—No. 2, lying from eight to twelve feet above No. 1, shows from twelve to eighteen inches of bright coal, but being too thin for working profitably in the presence of thicker seams; no openings have been made to fairly test its quality.

"*Third Seam.*—No. 3 lies between one hundred and fifty and two hundred feet further up the mountain, and shows from one to three feet of bright coal. No openings have been made upon it.

"*Other Seams.*—The remaining workable seams lie, according to Safford, at about the following elevation above No. 1, viz: No. 4, three feet thick at 470 feet; No. 5, from three to six feet thick from 800 to 850 feet; No. 8, from four to six feet thick at from 1,250 to 1,350 feet; No. 9 is six feet thick at from 1,600 to 1,700 feet. No openings have been made to any of these seams. Fragments of clean coal, apparently belonging to No. 4, were found in the wash of a mountain branch, as it made its appearance from beneath the huge tumbling masses of sandstone which fill the bottoms of all the hollows. If extensive mining should be undertaken here, the coal of these upper seams could readily be brought down by a tram road, for the construction of which the heavy timber of the mountain-side would furnish abundant material.

A fine exposure of coal is seen at Hatmakers, near the top, and beyond Cross Mountain, four feet thick.

"The argillaceous red hematite, locally known as Dyestone, is found in great abundance. Along the foot of the mountain to the northward, two seams, commonly exist, ranging from one to five feet in thickness, and of different hardness. Of these the harder has not been mined, having been found difficult of reduction in the small forges of the country. It is, however, readily reduced in a smelting furnace. The softer bed has been mined along its outcrop for many miles. The openings near Careyville have now caved in, but the old miners inform me that the seams have averaged from four to five feet in thickness.

"Openings recently made upon the hill between the old Carey residence and the sulphur spring, have exposed a net work of veins which are massed at one point so as to give a thickness of twenty-one feet of solid ore, but this is near the junction of the two axis of the elevation, as before described, and such thickness is only local.

"The first railroad cut above the station exposed the upper seam, with a thickness of about four feet, which may be fairly accounted the average thickness of the seam in this region. This ore should yield in a good furnace between 60 and 70 per cent of iron.

"Brown hematite (limonite) hydrated oxide of iron has been seen in considerable quantities at three points upon the slope of Cross Mountain, viz: at 326, at 787, and at 1,275 feet above the mouth of the coal mine. At the lower two beds the ore appears to be merely surface accumulations in the hollows among the edges of the underlying rocks, and is sometimes rather sandy. Small surface excavations have not yet shown any solid bed of ore, but the numerous large masses lying about on the surface would indicate the presence of bodies large enough to be of considerable value. At the highest level the ore contains fossil plants, and this, together with the structure of the fragments, would indicate that this is only the altered outcropping of a regular vein of impure carbonate of iron known as clay ironstone. The ore, as it occurs upon the surface, should yield from 25 to 30 per cent of iron. The clay ironstone itself occurs in thin laminæ in the dark shales above coal No. 2, but no considerable amount has been seen at any point. As it occurs here it should yield from 30 to 35 per cent of iron."

The Dyestone seam continues northwardly from Careyville, and the ore from it was mined for many years at Sharp's Forge, near Big Creek Gap. The seam here has of an average thickness of three feet. The lower side is soft and crumbling, the upper hard. Sometimes a thin seam of shale separates the two layers. Higher up on the mountain is another seam of ore, of a steel blue color, and very rich. It requires about 400 lbs. of ore to make 100 lbs. of bar iron as worked in the forge, leaving a large per centage of iron in the cinder. Two fires in this forge have the capacity of 2,000 lbs. per week. The charcoal from a cord of wood will make about 100 lbs. of iron.

Another forge, Baker's, six miles south-east, on Cedar Creek, works the ore from the same seam, with similar results.

COVE CREEK AND ELK FORK REGION.

Cove Creek heads up from Careyville northwestward, and the railway line having reached Elk Fork Gap, ten miles above, drops over into the valley of Elk Fork of the Cumberland, which it follows north, north-east and south, to the Kentucky State line—the whole distance from Careyville being about twenty-seven miles.

On the east of Cove Creek is Fork Mountain, which forms a steep barrier, with cliffs at the south end. On the west, a similar mountain side, broken by ravines, rises to the height of 2,000 feet or more, and gradually declines to Morrowville, ten miles distant, where it is cut by Poteet's Gap. Its prolongation makes one of the ranges of the Jellico Mountains. Between Cross Mountain and Fork Mountain is a narrow valley, with small patches of arable land.

An anticlinal fold comes out of Fork Mountain at an acute angle into the bed of Cove Creek, near where the fossil ore and limestone have been brought to the surface by an upthrow of the anticlinal of Sharp's Gap.

The ascent of the road from Careyville to Elk Gap tunnel is 450 feet, or at the rate of 45 feet per mile. The coal outcrops are at all elevations above the railway, from grade up to nearly 2,000 feet.

Prof. Lesley, in an unpublished report of this region, says:

"Most of the coal seams are at present inaccessible, only the lowest can be worked at Careyville. Moreover, much of the lower 1,000 feet is occupied by sand rocks, sandy shales, flagstone formations, and smaller coal beds. These occupy the terrace knobs of Careyville face of the mountain, and they make up the two barriers, right and left-hand of Cove Creek, up to the sixth or seventh mile. From this up the right-hand barrier (Fork Mountain) continues to consist of the same inferior measures; but the mountains on the left have the superior measure; and these take possession of the whole country to the west of Walker's and southwest of Elk Gap. The superior measures consist of 1,000 feet or less of soft shales, containing workable coal beds, with a great sand rock (Fortress Rock) below, and a great sand rock (Cap Rock) on top. The big coal bed lies just on the Fortress Rock, and outcrops nearly at water-level, seven feet thick, one-half mile west of Walker's, between the ninth and tenth miles. It can be mined all through the country to the west of this. Its outcrop on the other or eastern side of the anticlinal, is in the ravines back of Sharpe's Run Valley. It is worked by Sharpe, at a point half-a-mile north-east of his house, and at another point a mile and a-half south-east of his house. The valley of Cove Creek and Sharpe's Run are excavated in the great shale formation below the Fortress Rock and above the conglomerate (the sand rocks of the anticlinal) the one on the one side, the other on the other side of the anticlinal, exhibited by section A. B., thus: Fig. 1.

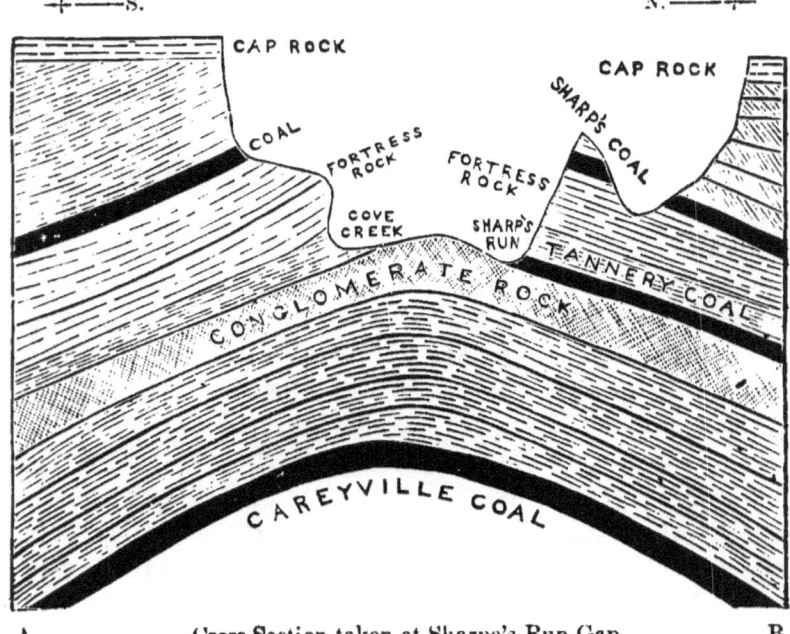

A   Cross Section taken at Sharpe's Run Gap.   B

"Further explanation is necessary. Only the upper part of Cove Creek valley is the more valuable. The Careyville lower coals are those under ground. The anticlinal apparently flattens out as it approaches the Elk Mountain, giving place to a gentle rise to the north-west of all the measures, bringing the concealed Careyville coals to view on the outside slope of the Elk Mountain. Their crops are noticeable in the road descending from the gap to the lime kiln, on the headbreaks of Elk Fork water. The descent is one of 350 feet vertical. At the lime kiln we come upon the top layers of the subcarboniferous limestone. In flattening, tne anticlinal rises northward from Sharpe's.

"In like manner, coming southward, the anticlinal rises slowly and spreads its two legs somewhat. Cove Creek can no longer keep in the shales above the anticlinal conglomerate rocks. It cuts slowly sidewise through the left (west) leg, and gets into the centre line of the anticlinal, between its two legs, and thus cuts down to the underlying coal system, or Careyville coals, which appear in the cuttings in the railway in many places—at least the rock at Sharpe's Run Gap gets to the top of the Knobs overlooking the saw-mill 350 feet above the creek, and 300 feet above the Careyville coal bed.

"But when the Cove Creek water has cut a rocky, narrow channel through the west leg of the anticlinal, and reached its axis about two miles above the saw-mill, the north-west dip opposite the second bridge is forty-five degrees, and in the neighborhood the water is seen flowing over nearly vertical shales and flagstones; and fossils, iron ore, and limestone, were found in the bed of the creek not far above the saw-mill.

"The anticlinal must, therefore, be considered as having snapped along its back, and let the whole of Cross Mountain drop, while the north-east bank of Cove Creek rose several thousand feet ,bringing iron ore to a level with the coal measures. The direction of this fissure must be N.W. and S. E., and the line of it must be under the pointed end of Fork Mountain. It is next to impossible to describe the method by which the ore could get into the valley. Two separate fractures of the crust of the earth seem necessary to explain it, meeting at a low angle just where the anticlinal axis ends, and bringing up a sharp wedge of the iron ore bearing rocks.

"The two branches of Sharpe's Run flow from different points of the compass, to meet at the place where the back of the anticlinal is lower than anywhere else, either further north or further south; and here the combined stream breaks through the anticlinal out of the shales of a shallow trough, in which they have been flowing into the same shales in the deeper trough of Cove Creek. They cannot there turn northwest for an outlet, because all the measures are gently rising in that direction.

"They, therefore, turn south with the drainage of that north-west district, keep the west side of the anticlinal as far as possible, and there. by some weak place produced by the neighboring fracture, get into and under the rocks of the anticlinal, find the soft rocks of the iron ore formation outcrops, and follow it and the fissure out into the open country."

Lesley further says in his report:

"We proved that there is no regularly workable bed in a thousand feet of measures from the Careyville coal bed up to the seven feet, or Sharpe's coal bed. I do not mean to say that at no place some one or other of these intermediate coal beds may not be workable. Local impediments in these beds are to be expected. On certain tracts one or other of them may become three or four feet thick, and, therefore, valuable. But as a rule, and so far as they are now known, they are not worth reporting upon. This is equally true of the beds beneath the (conglomerate?) anticlinal sand rocks, Nos. 5 and 4, and between that and the Careyville coal. Safford gives two such coal beds, and makes them both three feet, but it must be a mistake; for, in the first place, there are more than two, as the outcrops in the railroad cuttings, and up the hill slopes over the railroad, show; and, in the next place, not one of all these outcrops gives any hope of a workable bed. They are beds of poor coal and black slate mixed, and not thick enough for a gangway at that. The "lower" (3) coal shows in the road leading up from Careyville over the mountain, and is evidently thin, at the same time level. Just under the rocks of the Knob, over the saw-mill, its place is marked. The upper bed, however, has been used by the settlers, where it outcrops still higher up the mountain at the saw-mill, and is called three feet thick there. I do not know its thickness or quality, except by hearsay. These sub-conglomerate coals are always very variable and uncertain, expanding unexpectedly, and sometimes to an astonishing size.

"I have known an expansion of a five-foot bed to twenty-five feet in a few yards distance, but such deposits are entirely local.

"It is to be expected, therefore, that at some points these lower coals will be workable for short distances, but no reliance can be placed upon them. It would be unsafe to establish an extensive colliery on even the best exposures. To illustrate this, I shall now speak of the Careyville bed.

The Careyville bed is given by Safford, thus:

Shales...	10
Coal-top bench...	1
Shale and fire clay..	4
Shale...	5
Coal main seam	3
Fire clay..	6
Sandy shales visible for 30.	

"The extensive workings here during sixteen months have revealed the behavior of the bed. The two benches which compose it lie sometimes within two feet of each other, and at other times have sixteen feet of measures between them. At the little tangent next below the saw-mill, the interval is ten feet. Where they are three feet apart, the interval consists of slatery coal. The upper layer, or bed, is very regularly 16 feet thick, and first-rate coal. The main bed varies from three to one and a-half feet. These variations are sudden. At the saw-mill, in the ravine back of the railroad embankment, the bed outcrops with 3′—4″ of coal, and a gangway was driven in for a mine, but the coal nipped down to 18″ or 20″, and ran so for one hundred yards, where the mine was abandoned. These variations in the bed are essential to its original deposit, and not the result of the neighborhood of the fault."

Disposing of the lower coal seams as being comparatively unimportant, and showing very clearly that the Careyville coal belongs to these, and must be far below the seam worked at Coal Creek, Prof. Lesley proceeds to describe the upper coal system as developed on Cove Creek.

"The bed of most importance," says Prof. Lesley, "is the seven-feet bed, so called because Mr. Winter actually got a clean seven-foot cut across its undisturbed outcrop in the ravine, three-quarters of a mile west of Walker's house, and within a couple hundred yards of the creek, and but a few yards above its water-level.

"It outcrops behind a promontory, through which it descends with a dip of about ten degrees north-east, and it must basin in this promontory, and outcrops along its face. As the promontory rises down stream, the bed basins deeper into it, and spreads back into the hill. Whether it be an outlying basin, or one connected with the extension area of the bed in the mountain to the south-west, I had not time to determine. I place no particular value on this particular exposure beyond the fact that shows how conveniently the coal can be reached from the railroad, and the excellent character and condtitition of the bed. It shows a clean face of seven feet between the roof and floor, both visible, with scarcely a trace of slate; bituminous, bright, sufficiently solid.

Of course I do not expect this bed to be everywhere as thick and homogeneously good as it shows itself to be here. But it is reasonable to expect it to be a large bed over large areas. I shall new describe its appearance along its outcrops. East of Sharpe's Run, supposing it to be the same, and my reason for so supposing it expressed in diagram, figure 2, may however be mistaken in identifying the rock of the cliffs opposite the promontory with the Fortress Rock under Sharpe's bed. Should the rock of the cliffs prove to be one of the three, sand rocks below the Fortress Rock, then the seven-feet coal bed at this point will be identical with a so-called three-foot bed opened and mined by Sharpe in the bed of the run, a mile east of his house; and this would place the seven-feet bed one step lower in the series; but still far above the conglomerate of the anticlinal, it would only widen its area, and make its general position more convenient for reaching from the railway.

"It is, therefore, a practically unimportant uncertainty. I will proceed, however, on the supposition. The big bed of the series is the seven-feet bed just described."

"The country about Sharpe's coal mine is watered by rills, numerous and copious, issuing from the horizontal outcrops of these beds high up on the sides of the mountains. The upland is formed by horsebacks, or sharp wall-like zigzagging ridges, capped by the Cap Rock, which is about thirty feet thick. There are scarcely any sandstone layers visible in the seven hundred feet of interval between the Cap Rock and Fortress Rock. All is shale, sometimes highly ferruginous. Iron ore beds may occur, but cannot be of any any great value.

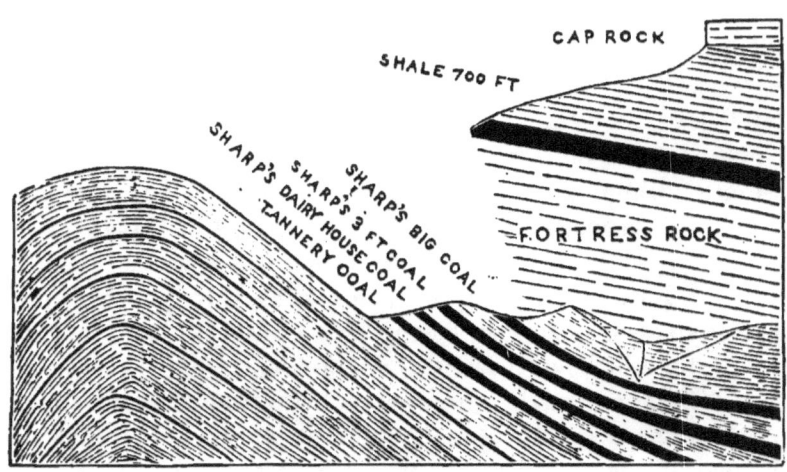

"The roof of Sharpe's coal is a good, hard shale, which will not give much trouble. The upper bench of coal has a sort of fire clay eight inches thick over it, which will bother the miners. The upper bench of coal is 3 1-12 feet thick where opened, and breaks up into horizontal laminæ at the outcrop, but becomes solid under the hill, breaking up vertically. It is hard, and extraordinarily free from foreign matter. I supposed it to be quite ashey from the appearance of the specimen. Analyzed by P. Frazier, jr., of the University of Pennsylvania, instructor of chemistry, it contained, according to analysis:

Water,	2.22
Volatile combustible matter,	31.15
Carbon, fixed,	64.32
Ash,	2.31
	100

Ashes, pulvurulent reddish brown.

By net analysis---Sulphur, ... 2.1

"A fire clay, only eight inches thick, separates this from

the middle bench of apparently much better coal, but which in reality shows almost an identical analysis:

Water,	0.77
Ash,	2.82
Volatile combustible matter,	31.58
Carbon, fixed,	64.83
	100

Ashes, pulvurulent pinkish gray.
By net analysis---Sulphur, ... 3.07

"The lower bench consists of nearly a foot and a-half of cannel coal in half-inch layers, not good enough for the market, but well adapted for fuel in the blast furnace when mixed with the purer coals of the upper and middle benches. In this sense the whole bed can be used. Between roof and floor there are sixty-eight inches sixty-six of which are coal."

"The two coal beds which occur in the midst of the 700 feet of shales beneath the Cap Rock were opened by Mr. Winter, in the hills south-west and south of the Elk Gap and Buckeye tavern. They are good looking, three and four feet beds, and will undoubtedly prove workable over extensive areas. A mile above the Buckeye, on the north side of Cove Creek, near its head, and close to the railroad line, Mr. Winter opened a three-foot and four-foot bed, a little contorted, he thought, with sand rock roof and fire clay floor, dipping twenty-five degrees north, sixty east. In fact, there cannot be any obstacle in the way of extensive and profitable mining along the valley of Cove Creek."

Passing now through Elk Gap, the divide between the waters of the Tennessee and the waters of the Cumberland, 1,702 feet above the sea, we descend gently to the Elk Fork Valley, drained by Elk Fork, a tributary of Clear Fork of the Cumberland. The valley of Elk Fork is fifteen miles in length, fourteen of which is in the State of Tennessee. It is deeply set in the Table-land, narrow, and bounded on the east by Pine Mountain, a high straight ridge, and on the west by the outlying knobs of Jellico Mountain. The existence of a great fault, by which a dislocation of strata, amounting, probably, to 2,000 feet, has made this valley one of peculiar interest to geologists, while the great extent and value of its coal and iron have given it a special interest to the iron master. By this dislocation all the strata from the eastern side, as low as the Trenton rocks of the lower Silurian, have been brought above the surface; while on the opposite side, facing these, are the carboniferous. From the line of fault the dip is backwards in opposite directions. At Alvan Smith's, four miles from the Kentucky line, a seam of coal, four feet thick, abuts against the limestone rocks, dipping westwardly 28 degrees under Elk Fork. This same seam has been opened at many places above and below. At places below it forms the bed of Elk Fork for a considerable distance.

The Clinton Group, including the fossil or Dyestone ore, has a great development in this valley. Descending the valley, we pass over the outcrops of two or three seams of coal, and find the limestone outcropping on the line of fault at the lime kiln. A half mile or more below this we first meet with the Clinton rocks. Prof. Lesley and Mr. Winter made a thorough survey of this region, a large portion of which is appended.

The descent from Elk Gap shows three seams of coal. "These coal beds," says Prof. Lesley, "are subconglomerate coals, and are probably the Careyville coal beds. They outcrop on the road, and evidently dip south or southeast into the Cove Creek country. I thought at first that the cliffs overhanging the gap were of the Fortress Rock, but the section shows that they correspond to the great sand rock, 200—300 feet vertically over the Careyville coal bed. The limestone appears at the lime kiln apparently turned up vertical by the great fault which points directly toward it, and swallows up the lower formations one by one until it leaves nothing but these top layers of the subcarboniferous limestone, visible on the side of the coal measure (Elk) mountain. As the fault runs off north and the mountain east of north-east, the whole of the subcarboniferous comes up out of the fault, and forms the lower half of the mountain slope for many miles, and, indeed, far into Kentucky.

"The Devonian sands and shales come out of the fault within the next 1,200 yards going north from the lime kiln, but are probably so crushed up by the fault that their fragments have been swept off, leaving a hole in the surface now filled up level with sand and mud, making the triangular meadows of the widow Davis' farm. Probably other fractures, springing out of the main dislocation, have helped to produce this effect. But beyond the meadows they rise and form a bold ridge one hundred fifty feet high, more or less. On the back side, or next slope of this hill, appear the red shales of formation V (Clinton), carrying the fossil ore. The road takes up over a low place back of the hill made by these red shales.

"Back of the red shales runs a ridge formed by the thin but hard sandstone, precisely like the ridge of sandstone in front of the fossil ore and red shales at the tunnel, two and a half miles south of Careyville. This sandstone is the Southern representative of the great formation which, in the Northern States, form the principal mountains—Kittatinny Mountain, at the Delaware Water Gap; the Blue Mountain, at Port Clinton; Harrisburg, Chambersburg, etc.; what is there one thousand feet thick is here only twenty or thirty feet thick, but it maintains its relative position as the supporting rock of the red shales which carry the fossil ore, just as it does in the ridge, where the Danville mines are on its peak, and in the Bald Eagle mountains, where the Hollidaysburg ore mines are on its slope, and at Cumberland, etc. I made no explorations back of this ridge to see whether the slates of No. III, and the limestone of the great valley No. II, came up to occupy any of the surface; but I judge by the topography, as seen from a distance, that they stay underground, for Mr. Winter, who went back to find coal, says that the peak, half a mile west of the road consists of coal measures, and of course lies on the other side of the dislocation (the western or down-throw side).

"The first place where the red shales are seen coming up from the fault is about eight hundred paces north of the lime kiln, in the road two hundred yards beyond the little house on the left-hand side of the road. There is no use in looking for ore between the gap (or lime kiln) and this point. But shafts sunk at the south-west corner of the meadows should strike it, as it pitches steeply south sixty degrees east under the mountain; 240 paces beyond this point, or about 1,100 paces from the lime kiln, the red shale begins to form a low ridge, dipping forty-one degrees, and just behind, or under it, is the sandstone which forms the backbone of the ridge, while the red shale makes a terrace facing the road. One hundred steps further on the great ore bed rises from the meadow, and faces this terrace, with a wall of ore dipping sixty-six degrees south sixty-two degrees east.

"The beds *a* and *b* are simple plates of the pure ore one foot four inches and one foot five inches thick, separated by two inches of yellow shale, or clay. The beds *c, d* and *e*, are partially concealed by their own soil and the stuff that has slipped from the terrace of the red shale above, but enough is seen to convince one that a good portion of this interval, if not the whole of it, consists of plates of ore similar to *a* and *b*, with similar partings of clay. The bed *e* is excellent ore, a foot or more thick, standing in a plate like *a* and *b*, and under it is seen the face of another plate, *f*, the thickness of which is entirely concealed by soil. From the front face of *a* to the front face of *f* measures at right angles to both, strike and dip just twenty feet.

"It will be safe to take the whole twenty feet into the calculation of quantity, because the clay partings will go into the furnace with the plate ore as flux, only diminishing the per cent of metal. There does not appear to be any marked difference of quality in the different layers and pieces taken from the outcrop, are also exactly alike those taken from these plates. There is great uniformity in the ore wherever I have seen it, except that some specimens show the small crinoidal fossils abundantly, others sparingly, and some not at all.

"I can see no essential variation of quality when specimens of the ore from this outcrop are compared with specimens of the ore from the outcrop in the Careyville railroad tunnel, fifteen miles distant.

"Mr. Winter and I followed the outcrops of the ore 3,000 yards to Mr. Lewis Stanfield's house, and Mr. Winter a mile or two further, to where the valley narrows, and the coal mountains approach so close together that there is only room for the Elk Fork to flow in a deep gorge. There all the lower formations seem to have been again swallowed up in the fault (or in another fault of a similar character, with a more north-easterly course), and the ore is wholly under ground. After my return home Mr. Winter reports that he discovered the existence of two other beds of ore at the point of the hill on the right hand side of the road on the bank of the creek, the lower ore one foot thick, the upper ore three feet thick, solid ore, and these two beds not far apart. He also reports the great bed to be fifteen feet thick where it appears beyond the road-crossing of the little creek which comes in from the north-west.

"The difference between this measurement and that of the exposed wall of ore, *a*, *b*, and *d f*, was one to be expected. I have no idea that the big bed will run twenty-feet thick for any great distance. We are acquainted with the Clinton fossil ore of No. 5, along one hundred miles of the Appalachian mountains, and even ten feet is an exceptional thickness—twenty feet is something enormous, and quite abnormal. At the same time this thickness of fifteen or twenty feet gives an extraordinary value to this farm of the widow Davis, for the cliff in which it appears, will yield, at this one spot above water-level on the road side, 5,000 cubic yards, or 10,000 tons, of ore. An open quarry one hundred yards long and twenty feet deep, will afford a second 10,000 tons of ore, and so on.

"But the moment quarrying below water-level commences the bed becomes continous, and may be opened for three hundred yards as well as for one hundred. There is, also, no practical limit to its depth; instead of twenty feet, the miners may go down, by a single shaft, sixty or one hundred yards. A block twenty feet thick, sixty yards deep, and one hundred yards long, holds nearly a hundred thousand tons of ore.

"Crossing the little run, and entering the hill over which the road passes northward, the bed can be mined with a maximum breasting above the water-level of 70 feet, and if the bed runs at an average of only 10 feet through this hill eight hundred yards, with an average breasting of thirty feet there can be taken out of a horizontal gangway, 50,000 tons.

"It is needless to say more as to quantity. Besides this, must be taken into consideration the three feet beds above it.

"The next place where the ore is plainly visible, is in the field, to the left of the road, where it crosses the little hill, 1,700 yards (one mile) beyond the widow Davis's ore bank; across this field two broad bands of red soil run parallel to each other, and to the road, fifty paces asunder. In these red soil bands lies abundance of loose pieces of the ore. How thick the beds may be I do not see, but they are lineal continuations of the big bed (Davis's), and the two small beds above it.

"After my return Mr. Winter found that the bed next the road (the upper bed) was six feet thick, and the bed below it, where it was 120 yards from the road, was nine feet thick. This again gives one thousand tons of ore for every one hundred yards of surface-length of ore bed one yard deep. Along here the ore bed outcrops nowhere more than thirty feet above water-level, but that gives ten thousand tons of ore above water-level for every one hundred or one hundred and fifty yards of outcrop.

" Here Mr. Winter's opening showed that the ore bed took a more gentle slant, which was evident, also, otherwise from the mere inspection of the topography of the country. The dip is thirty-two degrees to the south, forty degrees east. The direction here found must be quite local, for the general strike of the outcrop is not far from north forty degrees east, south forty degrees west.

" In the road bank below Lewis Stanfield's, the nephew's house, five hundred paces further than the last mentioned place, a small bed of ore is seen dipping forty or fifty degrees to the south-east; two hundred and fifty yards further on an ore bed crosses the road.

"Between this point and Lewis Stanfield's, the uncle's house, the black shales (of VIII), overlying the ore, appear in the road.

" In the flat back of Stanfield's back yard, the lower ore crop runs along the ground, and shows plenty of crop fragments. Beyond this point I did not trace it.

" The above description will suffice to prove that millions of tons of fossil ore can be mined from these outcrops. Several hundred thousand tons above water-level, and the rest below it by shafts and slopes; the waste in mining will be small. The beds lie favorably for deep mining, and mining will not be expensive. Coal for smelting and charcoal can be obtained in any quantity from the neighborhood. The mountains are covered with forest. Mineral coal can be run over the railroad from Cove Creek, or beds can be opened in the high peaks and ridges from three-fourths of a mile to two miles east of the outcrops. Mr. Winter opened a coal bed two and a half feet thick in the mountain, the bed dipping in a westerly direction away from the fault. There is abundance of room for furnaces, plenty of rich farming land around, and miles of limestone within easy reach. But the line of the railroad must be entirely changed if ironworks are to be built and run successfully in this valley. The bed of the Elk Fork is low and swampy, and at the present located line, high up on the mountain side. By keeping down along the slopes of the mountains north-west of the lime kiln, and west of the outcrops of ore, the five hundred feet descent can be made with a loss of two miles of railroad distance only, and the road will come out upon the ore belt, and keep down over the fields on the west side of the Fork."

ANALYSIS OF THE ORE OF ELK FORK VALLEY.

Some singular features are presented in the analysis of this ore. It is quite variable in its chemical composition. It will be noticed that the ore is designated by plates a, b, c, and d, etc., each one of which shows some variation. It does not show as much metallic iron as that taken from Kindrick's and Rockwood, but the fact that it carries sufficient carbonates to flux itself is an important item in its favor. Indeed, Prof. Lesley thinks sand and clay will be needed in some cases as a flux. In regard to its analysis Prof. Lesley says:

"The fossil ore is cold-short from phosphorus in the common blast furnace, when high pressure and hot blast were used, but when used with low pressure and cold blast in small stacks, running from 1,000 to 1,500 tons of pig metal per annum, this ore makes excellent soft iron. In the Catalan forge it has always made superior metal.

"Made in large quantities it makes first quality hard rolled iron for heads of rails. If large quantities of pig iron are to be made in large hot blast stacks, it will be absolutely necessary to mix this fossil ore with the red short or neutral brown hematites (pipe ores) of the limestone valleys east of Careyville district. Powell's Valley has them also.

"In the analysis made by Dr. Gentle, the variable quantities of iron, lime, and phosphorus are remarkable.

	Specimen No. 1.	Specimen No. 2.
Ironstone	0.54	0.82
Silicia acid	6.46	9.70
Carbonic acid	19.87	10.92
Phosphoric acid	4.09	1.20
Ferric acid	39.96	59.94
Manganous oxide	0.37	0.32
Alumnia	2.13	1.90
Magnesia	6.49	4.55
Lime	20.19	10.65
	100.00	100.00
Metallic iron	27.97	41.96

"A small quantity of iron is present as ferrous carbonate, the balance as ferrous oxide, the phosphoric acid as bone phosphate of lime. The balance of the lime, the manganous oxide, the magnesia are in combination with carbonic acid.

"It will be noticed that as the iron (or oxide of iron) increases, the phosphoric acid diminishes, and the carbonic acid and lime also. This shows that the presence of phosphorus is due to the fossil shells in the ore. A resident chemist will be indispensable to iron works erected here, because every charge will have to be analyzed—every stratum in the bank must be tested before quarrying or mining proceeds. In no other way can this ore be used on a very extensive scale, for large, high power hot blast furnaces, making five to ten thousand tons of pig iron per year. In the low blast cold charcoal furnaces, or in the warm blast coke furnace where the heat is kept low, this ore will carry off its phosphoric acid in the cinder, and make excellent iron.

"The almost entire absence of alumina in the ore, or, rather, its replacement by magnesia, is very noteworthy, although not remarkable, because the rocks of lower silurian age from which the waters of the Clinton age flowed into the sea, are magnesian limestone. We should expect, therefore, very little sand or clay (silicic acid, or alumina), and large quantities of carbonate of lime, and carbonate of magnesia. The proper flux for this ore will, therefore, be, not limestone, but sand and clay, or any rock which consists of silica and alumina. If such a rock should contain carbon it would be all the more valuable—1st, by adding to the furnace fuel; 2nd, by being all the more fissile, falling to pieces in descending from the tunnel head. Such a rock is the so-called black band and heavy cannel coal of the coal measures, which are nearly common black slate charged with an unusual amount of iron. Mr. Winter found some black band near the head of Cove Creek. There is plenty of it to be found here and there in the hills of the Cove Creek region. It is not at all the "black band" of Scotland, and cannot be used for ore by itself as a burden for a blast furnace, but it consists of silica and alumina, with a heavy charge of carbon, or petroleum, and a variable, but always low percentage of iron. It is exactly what is wanted for fluxing this fossil ore. Cannel coal will act as well as a flux as a fuel for this ore, the higher its percentage of ash, or, in other words, the lower its heating power as fuel, the better will it serve as a flux. Forming with the magnesia and lime the multiple silicate of iron, lime, alumina, and magnesia, in which the phosphoric acid will pass off, or the worst of it, in its original form of phosphate of lime."

Such are the main portions of Prof. Lesley's report, the truth of which I verified by going over the whole field. That there is a great abundance of coal and iron ore lying convenient to each other cannot be questioned. With proper means of communication this Elk Fork valley will become famous for its iron manufactories. In a healthy and fertile region, where abundant supplies may be drawn from Powell's Valley, and from the numerous smaller valleys that make up part of the valley of East Tennessee, capital only is wanting to make this spot rival in industrial activity any place in the South or South-west. Elk Fork valley, with Cove Creek, cuts a quadrilateral block from the coal field.

The soil of Elk Fork valley is inclined to be cold and "crawfishy." Moderate yields of the principal field crops, however, are grown. The farms are much neglected, many of them being rented out every year. Very little clover is grown, and the land is cropped year after year without rest, and often without rotation. A considerable trade is carried on in dried fruit, eggs, butter, feathers, and beeswax. A few mules and cattle are raised, and driven out to Careyville. The farmers raise no money crop, though some of the land is well suited for tobacco. Lumber is abundant and cheap, selling at prices varying from ten to fifteen dollars per thousand. A considerable amount of walnut timber is found in the coves of the mountains. Poplar, oak, chestnut, and beech, are abundant. Sugartree and hackberry occur in the mountains. Chestnut oak is usually found on the highest points.

Passing out of Elk Fork valley westward by David's Fork, the country is very wild, but well timbered. Upon the higher mountain slopes the soil is fertile, and produces grain crops as well as the lands in the valley. Nimblewill grows on all the open places, and supplies excellent grazing for cattle. At Markham's Gap the low divide between the head-waters of David's Fork, and Smith's creek, which enters into Buffalo, this grass is very abundant. Walnut is found in considerable quantities near this gap.

Markham's Mountain, in which this gap occurs, is a part of Buffalo Mountain, belonging to the Jellico range. It lies between the east and west forks of Smith's creek, ten miles east of Huntsville. On the western slope of this mountain a section was taken which shows eight seams of coal. The following is an approximation of the thickness of the strata, the coal being measured with a rule, and the thick strata with a barometer. Beginning at top, we have,

Surface	220	feet.
Sandstone	40	"
Coal	10	inches.
Fire clay	3.6	
Hard blue sandy shale	25	feet.
Thin bedded sandstone	10	inches.
Gray shale	1.6	
Coal	3	inches.
Fire clay	13	"
Gray shale	15	feet.
Coal	1.6	
Fire clay	.6	
Sandy shale	12	feet.
Coal	2	inches.
Shale	2	feet.
Shaly sandstone	8	feet.
Black shale	1.6	
Coal	2.3	
Gray shale	6.	
Fire clay	1.8	
Coal	1.3	
Hard sandy shale	11	feet.
Coal	1.6	
Gray shale	12	feet.
Coal	6	inches.
Shale and sandstone	394	feet.
Coal	6	inches.

It will be seen that by far the larger number of seams is thin and worthless, only one or two being workable. The thickness would, doubtless, increase beyond the outcrop.

The soil in the valley of Buffalo is very fertile, and a considerable amount of corn is grown, and many cattle raised and driven out. On Trammel's Fork of Smith's Fork the valley is trough-like, but the slopes of the mountains are very productive. As fine timber as can be found in the State grows upon the slopes, of almost all valuable varieties found in the State. The soil is very black and friable. At some places it is difficult to ride on account of the looseness of the soil. The capabilities of these mountain slopes are almost unknown. Cultivated by an intelligent Swiss population, they could be made as attractive as any portion of the State. And this is true of all the north--eastern part of Scott county—a county of great possibilities, and one that is certain to grow in wealth, enterprise, and population, when the several lines of railroad now proposed shall have been completed.

www.ingramcontent.com/pod-product-compliance
Lightning Source LLC
Chambersburg PA
CBHW030345170426
43202CB00010B/1250